PIERS BRENDON

# Edward VIII

## The Uncrowned King

PENGUIN BOOKS

PENGUIN BOOKS

UK | USA | Canada | Ireland | Australia
India | New Zealand | South Africa

Penguin Books is part of the Penguin Random House group of companies
whose addresses can be found at global.penguinrandomhouse.com.

First published by Allen Lane 2016
First published in Penguin Books 2018

001

Copyright © Piers Brendon, 2016

The moral right of the author has been asserted

Set in 9.5/13.5 pt Sabon LT Std
Typeset by Jouve (UK), Milton Keynes
Printed and bound in Great Britain by Clays Ltd, Elcograf S.p.A.

ISBN: 978-0-141-98735-4

www.greenpenguin.co.uk

# Contents

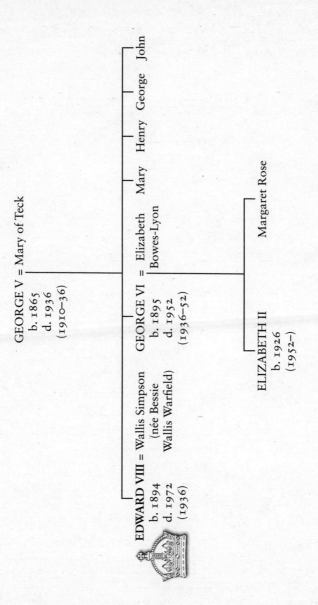

EDWARD VIII = Wallis Simpson
b. 1894      (née Bessie
d. 1972      Wallis Warfield)
(1936)

GEORGE V = Mary of Teck
b. 1865
d. 1936
(1910–36)

GEORGE VI = Elizabeth
b. 1895      Bowes-Lyon
d. 1952
(1936–52)

Mary    Henry    George    John

ELIZABETH II
b. 1926
(1952–)

Margaret Rose

*Edward VIII*

# I
# Royal Destiny

Edward VIII reigned for less than a year and was never crowned king. Far from fulfilling the splendid destiny proclaimed as his birthright, he shook the Windsor dynasty, newly established in 1917, by abdicating to marry the divorced woman he loved. The event had been foretold in two memorable prophecies. The first was by the pioneer socialist Keir Hardie. It was provoked by Parliament's refusal to add to its congratulatory address on the birth of Prince Edward, which took place on 23 June 1894, an expression of sympathy for more than 250 Welsh miners killed in a colliery explosion on the same day. Hardie declared, amid cries of 'Oh! Oh!' and 'Order!', that from childhood

> this boy will be surrounded by sycophants and flatterers by the score and will be taught to believe himself as of a superior creation ... In due course ... he will be sent on a tour round the world, and probably rumours of a morganatic alliance will follow, and the end of it all will be the country will be called upon to pay the bill.[1]

Edward's father, plagued in his final years by worries about his son's infatuation, was equally prescient. Where others saw a star, George V saw a meteor, and he predicted that after he was dead 'the boy will ruin himself within twelve months'.[2] Certainly Edward's renunciation of the throne damaged the monarchy. It led to a schism between the Duke of Windsor, as Edward then became, and the new sovereign, his brother George VI. It made divorce such a royal taboo that Princess Margaret was unable to wed the man of her choice in 1955 and a generation later it cast a long shadow over Prince Charles's marital affairs. It also put a premium on sovereign responsibility and propriety, as embodied by Queen Elizabeth II. Her reign, like that of her father, can be seen as an attempt to exorcize the ghost of the abdication. Only a lifetime dedicated to duty could efface memories of Edward VIII's short, unhappy kingship. It was the louring meridian in a career whose morning was golden and whose afternoon was leaden.

The pit disaster aside, the auguries could hardly have been more favourable at Edward's nativity. He was the great-grandson of Queen Victoria and, as the eldest son of the Duke of York, the heir to Edward (VII) Prince of Wales, he stood in direct line of succession to the throne. The queen herself was not only the 'grandmother of Europe', her descendants dominating the courts of the continent, but the Empress of India, presiding over a Greater Britain on which the sun never set. As the first industrial nation and a commercial colossus with a pre-eminent navy, her tiny offshore island was the greatest power on earth. At home she basked in the quasi-religious loyalty of her people. And when the queen's might and majesty were celebrated at her Golden and Diamond

Jubilees, she was said to have become 'visibly transfigured before the eyes of her subjects'.[3] Between these two patriotic festivals Edward was born at White Lodge, Richmond Park, the home of his mother's parents, the Duke and Duchess of Teck. A month later, in the presence of the queen and many notabilities, he was baptized by the Archbishop of Canterbury from a golden bowl of Jordan water, and christened Edward Albert Christian George Andrew Patrick David. The first three names identified him with royal relations while the last four were those of the patron saints of England, Scotland, Ireland and Wales. The prince's arrival was greeted with expressions of joy and devotion in all corners of the United Kingdom, echoed throughout the empire. Clergymen attributed the glorious summer to the advent of this son of York. *The Times* intoned that he was the beneficiary of a noble inheritance and, plainly confident that its voice would be heard in regions above, prayed that he would be worthy of so great a trust.

In royal matters appearances are especially liable to deceive, and the expectations of this newspaper, which became Edward VIII's most voluble critic during the abdication crisis, were to be dashed on the rocks of reality. For nurture and nature would so conspire to make the most popular, glamorous and widely travelled Prince of Wales in history unfit to wear the crown – in his own estimation as well as that of others. David, as his family always called him, received an upbringing that, for all its fairy-tale facade, was narrow and loveless even by Victorian standards. His mother, then the Duchess of York and later

Queen Mary, was shy, stiff and bloodless, a jewelled automaton. To be sure, she sometimes displayed affection towards her children – David, her buttercup-blond favourite, was joined by Bertie (later King George VI) in 1895, Mary (later the Princess Royal) in 1897, Henry (later Duke of Gloucester) in 1900, George (later Duke of Kent) in 1902, and Prince John (who was epileptic and possibly autistic) in 1905. But hugs and kisses were in short supply at home. There was no 'passionate tenderness'[4] and in public a glacial formality prevailed. When the queen died in 1953 her eldest son unforgettably told his wife, 'I'm afraid the fluids in her veins have always been as icy cold as they now are in death.'[5] By contrast David's father, who seemed like a genial squire devoted to shooting and stamp-collecting, was a splenetic martinet. An old seadog himself, he growled and barked at his children. He imposed a stern domestic discipline and enjoined strict adherence to old-fashioned standards, particularly in dress and protocol. Errant offspring were chivvied, snubbed, baited, bullied and beaten. David would later tell his cousin Lord Mountbatten that he envied him a father whom he could love: 'If my father had died, we should have felt nothing but relief.'[6]

David spent much of his childhood immured in his father's cherished home York Cottage, which Edward VII had built on the Sandringham estate to accommodate additional guests at his shooting parties. With its small rooms and thin walls York Cottage was compared to a suburban villa or a seaside boarding house, but it was actually quite commodious. Moreover David and his siblings were often invited to Sandringham House itself, whose ugliness was only surpassed by its luxury. Here they were spoilt by their grandparents, learning crocheting from Queen Alexandra and sliding bits of buttered toast down the seams of King Edward's trousers. Still, York Cottage was a place of confinement. Life in the nursery was restrictive, painfully so in David's case, since a vicious nanny pinched him to make him howl before presenting him to his parents at teatime, doubtless to demonstrate her capacity to calm him afterwards – eventually she was discovered and dismissed.

Life in the schoolroom was equally constrained. Under the auspices of a games-playing prep-schoolmaster, Henry Hansell, the royal children underwent the grind of instruction without acquiring the benefit of education. David had a quick brain (especially in comparison with his stammering brother Bertie), an enquiring mind and an exceptionally retentive memory for facts and faces. But he took little interest in the standard subjects he was taught – languages, literature, history, geography, maths – and he seemed positively allergic to print. In later years he seldom read books, repeating the sad mantra of the unlettered that he preferred to learn from life. The stifling philistinism of York Cottage was partly to blame for all this. Despite the availability of an Aladdin's Cave of royal treasures, many of them looted from the empire, its rooms were furnished by Maples and its walls decorated with hoary maxims such as 'A Stitch in Time Saves Nine'. Queen Mary, it is true, did value *objets d'art*, particularly those that augmented regal prestige, and she was not above purloining them; but when George V heard the word 'culture' he reached, metaphorically at least, for his gun. He thought authors should be shut up, shook his stick at a Cézanne and confused highbrow with eyebrow. Despite the privileges of his exalted station, David grew up in a tight social circle and straitened intellectual circumstances.

His youth, though, was not all harsh discipline. It was enlivened by impromptu outdoor sports and games of ludo and canasta. It was palliated by servants (whom the royal children in some ways came to resemble, especially in modes of speech) and David was long sustained by the loyalty of his personal retainer Frederick Finch. He attended dancing classes, a rare chance to meet contemporaries. On the golf course he caddied for his father. He and his siblings sang folk songs and played soldiers. They also indulged in high jinks and practical jokes, once inducing their French tutor to eat an exotic savoury which actually consisted of tadpoles on toast. However David's father was determined that he and Bertie should undergo the rigours of naval training. This was an odd decision, since he recognized how poorly his own apprenticeship afloat had equipped him for sovereignty. Yet it was based on faith in the Senior Service's capacity to form the character of future leaders and it reflected the hope that encountering other boys on equal terms (the first time this royal experiment had been tried) would prepare the young princes to take their place in an increasingly democratic realm.

So in 1907 the twelve-year-old David, assured by his father that 'I am your best friend',[7] was packed off in tears and in brass-buttoned blue uniform to the Naval College at

Osborne on the Isle of Wight. Here he endured a regime of cold baths, hard beds, bad food and shouted orders carried out at the double. Stiff punishments were compounded by bullying, including, in David's case, a mock guillotining. Nicknamed 'Sardine', a tribute to his slight frame and maybe an adolescent pun on his impending metamorphosis as Prince of Wales, he was doubtless shielded from the worst kinds of abuse. And Osborne was no more brutal and boorish than many public schools of the day. Nevertheless it must have come as a severe shock to him. He performed indifferently at work, learning knots and picking up the rudiments of seamanship – he later warned that no one should sail in a ship which relied on him for navigation. Indeed, the best that can be said of his career at Osborne was that he shone in comparison to his knock-kneed brother Bertie, who was tongue-tied with his fellows and slow-witted in class, regularly coming bottom. David was unable to help him much since, as a senior cadet, he was prohibited from talking to a junior.

David himself became a junior again when he progressed to Dartmouth in 1909, but by this time he was inured to communal living and could make friends more easily. Moreover the Naval College's fine new premises overlooking the Dart estuary were less Spartan than those of Osborne and he enjoyed more freedom. However bullying was still rife and the curriculum was hardly calculated to broaden David's mental horizons. Moreover his studies were interrupted by royal events, notably the visit of Tsar Nicholas II and the death of King Edward VII on 6 May 1910. The monarch's passing caused personal sadness, national mourning, funereal pomp, political strain and domestic upheaval – King George V moved into Buckingham Palace, Windsor Castle and Balmoral, though he kept up York Cottage since Queen Alexandra occupied Sandringham until her death in 1925. The dynastic order also changed.

David was now heir apparent, his position sustained by vast wealth, mainly in revenues from property in south London and the West Country, which he inherited as Duke of Cornwall. On his sixteenth birthday the new monarch created him Prince of Wales. This obliged him to take a more prominent ceremonial role, which he found increasingly tedious, spurious and odious. Wearing the feathered hat and robes of the newly bestowed Order of the Garter over a cloth-of-silver costume at King George's coronation in 1911, he knelt before his father and vowed to become his 'liege man of life and limb . . . against all manner of folks'.[8] David revolted, though, at the prospect of his investiture as Prince of Wales in Caernarfon Castle. This was a pseudo-archaic pageant cynically devised by David Lloyd George (who complained that King George's court 'reeks with Toryism')[9] to exploit royalty for his own political purposes. And it required the Prince of Wales to dress up in white satin breeches and a mantle and surcoat of crimson velvet trimmed with ermine. He would be ridiculed by his naval friends, he protested, in this 'preposterous rig'.[10] Obliged to submit, the prince parroted a few words of Welsh and acted out the charade with dignity and grace.

After completing his naval training, as a midshipman during an autumn cruise on the battleship *Hindustan*,

David underwent a 'finishing' programme in preparation for his future role. While his parents sailed to India for the coronation durbar he was supposed to swot for Oxford but often broke off to assist Queen Alexandra with jigsaw puzzles and games of patience. He practised shooting and enjoyed it, though once, when conspicuously failing to match his father's expertise, he denounced the sport as 'an old woman's game'.[11] He paid a four-month visit to France, chaperoned by Henry Hansell and others, where he imbibed little of the culture and less of the language but played a lot of golf and tennis and attended frequent race meetings. He inspected his estates and sought a private secretary to help manage them – the Tory civil servant J. C. C. Davidson refused this courtier role, not being 'a yes-man or a lickspittle' and not quite liking the 'charming' prince, whom he later described as 'an obstinate, but really a weak man'.[12]

Certainly Prince Edward, as he must now be called, was young for his age when he arrived at Magdalen College in October 1912. Boyish in appearance and retarded by his upbringing, he made little progress in learning although individually tutored by the most eminent scholars in the university, including Magdalen's ineffably snobbish President, Herbert Warren. Isolated by rank and privilege, the royal freshman found it hard to fit into student society. He oscillated between encouraging familiarity and requiring deference. The prince told undergraduates who stood up when he first entered the Junior Common Room that he didn't want to be treated ceremoniously, but when they remained seated on his next visit he charged them with disrespect to the heir to the throne. On another occasion Edward allowed a fellow golfer to use his family name, but when he did so in front of others the prince abandoned the game and the friendship. However his ready smile, his debonair manner, his angelic looks and above all the charisma of his caste dazzled most of his contemporaries. Among them, it is recorded, was 'a rampant tearing Socialist from the Midlands' who responded to the prince's cheery toast, 'Here's luck, everybody,' by raising his glass to 'The Prince of Wales, God bless him!'[13]

With great gusto Edward also joined in many Oxonian recreations. He played football, cricket and squash. Although still nostalgic for the navy, he drilled and camped with the Officers' Training Corps. Nervously he attended a debate at the Union, biting his nails and looking 'virginally awkward'.[14] After initial resistance he took riding lessons and soon became a keen and bold horseman. He beagled, hunted, punted, ran with the college boat and scorched in his new 39-horsepower Daimler. He smoked and gambled. As well as giving spirited entertainments in his own rooms, he drank to excess, amid the breaking of glass and the smashing of furniture, at the Bullingdon Club. He also practised on his banjo, provoking protesters to gather beneath his window. He put them to flight with a skirl on the bagpipes, which he played with even less skill, sounding like a dying cow.

Despite all this the prince did not much enjoy Oxford. He was still under the eye of Henry Hansell and the king kept carping about his conduct and nagging him on a subject that mightily preoccupied them both – clothes. In matters of dress, as in other matters, King George was conventional to the point of ossification. He never missed or tolerated a sartorial solecism and when dining with him in private the prince had to wear a white tie and tails plus his star and garter. The prince himself favoured less starchy garb, his preferences running to flannel shirts, sports coats, loud checks, red tartans and baggy plus-fours. Fancying himself 'a bit of a dandy',[15] he tried to start a vogue for blue bowlers, which did not catch on. He also wore trousers with turn-ups. This fashionable novelty provoked paroxysms of monarchical fury and sarcastic questions about whether the royal apartments were wet or muddy. When obliged to conform, Edward was liable to subvert decorum by giving his top hat a rakish tilt. Here was a juvenile manifestation of what one historian has called his 'trivial revolt'[16] against the established order.

It was equally apparent in Germany, which he visited twice during the spring and summer vacations of 1913. There he met many of his royal relations, including the Kaiser, who donned one histrionic uniform after another and pronounced his guest to be 'a young eagle, likely to play a big part in European affairs'.[17] But the prince was indifferent to his kin and bored by the official entertainments staged for him. He did evince an interest in German automobiles, warships and dirigibles. But he reserved most enthusiasm for Berlin, which provided his first real experience of louche nightlife and proved that the Palace was much less fun than the *Palais de Danse*. Down from Oxford without regret and undergoing military training in preparation for joining the Grenadier Guards, he whirled his way vigorously through the last London Season before the war. He also undertook his first public engagements, performing appealingly on his own and receiving a foretaste of the adulation that would later engulf him. But he became increasingly resentful about the constraints of court etiquette. In a passage often quoted from his diary, he inveighed against the 'unreal show & ceremony' in which he had to participate during the state visit of the King and Queen of Denmark: 'What rot & a waste of time, money, & energy all these State visits are!!'[18]

This irritation was as nothing to the anguish the Prince of Wales endured when he was prohibited from fighting in the First World War. Courage was his salient virtue and he burned with martial ardour. But unlike legions of youth who rushed to the colours, he was denied a combatant role. King George, Lord Kitchener and others in authority believed that it would be a national disaster if the heir to the throne were killed or, perhaps even worse, captured. Not everyone agreed: Lord Hugh Cecil told the Archbishop of Canterbury that the prince ought to go to the Front because 'people won't like the King not risking anything'.[19]

However, after being commissioned into the Grenadier Guards, he was at first stationed at home and then, in response to his vehement protests, sent to France in November 1914 but kept well behind the lines. He was given staff jobs, first with Sir John French, commander-in-chief of the British Expeditionary Force, and later with Lord Cavan, who became commander-in-chief of British forces on the Italian Front. But he rightly assumed that these posts were designed to prevent him from seeing action and complained that he was the one unemployed man in northern France. In fact he did occasionally manage to get into the battle zone, experiencing the terror as well as the horror of trench warfare, and in 1915 a shell killed his chauffeur. But Edward continued to agonize over his uselessness, giving way to moods of self-pity and self-laceration. His lack of proper occupation, he said, made him feel a worm and a swine. In the lewd argot of the army, he cursed his fate. He thought he was going mad and contemplated suicide. He mortified his flesh by eating little and taking violent exercise, often eschewing the royal Daimler for a heavy green army bicycle. Nothing emphasized his unworthiness more than being promoted to Captain and awarded the Military Cross. He was ashamed to wear the decoration, normally bestowed for acts of conspicuous gallantry, earning another paternal rebuke.

Actually the Prince of Wales made a greater contribution to the war effort than he realized, notably in boosting military morale. The sincere admiration he felt for fighting soldiers was clearly apparent on his tours of inspection, as was his unaffected compassion for the wounded during hospital visits. His 1916 trip to the Middle East, nominally to report on the defences of the Suez Canal, was also productive. Although churlishly dismissing Anzac troops as bloody fools for cheering his arrival, he quickly developed a marked respect for them, which strengthened their imperial loyalties and his own. He was also credited with fortifying Sudanese allegiance, though he disliked being lionized in Khartoum and shared his grandfather's aversion to 'tumble-down' old temples on the Nile.[20] In fact he thrilled to nothing but snake charmers and old soldiers who had fought 'the maddened Fuzzy-Wuzzies' responsible for the death of General Gordon.[21] Back in France the prince supported the newly established rest, recreation and religious centre known as Toc H.

Although kept away from the carnage on the Somme, training instead in the use of aviation, artillery and other military techniques, he did witness preparations for the Battle of Passchendaele, which he described as the nearest possible thing to hell. Here his wish to share the sacrifice of front-line troops was nearly granted when his observation post came under fire. But in November 1917 he accompanied Lord Cavan's XIV Army Corps to north Italy, where the enemy threatened to break through after their victory at Caporetto. It was hoped that the prince would put heart into a shattered ally and he did his best, notably on a successful diplomatic visit to Rome, while privately disparaging spaghetti, Chianti, Venice, the pope ('a dirty little priest') and the people ('Ice-creamers'), and thanking heaven that he himself was 'not of a Latin race'. On his return to another staff appointment in France, in May 1918, he was happier attempting to inspire Canadians and Americans. Despite what he took to be their boastfulness, the prince formed a strong bond with them, particularly through 'talking filth ... I have to pretend to have the dirtiest mind of all, to keep them going'.[22] That aside, he warmed to their bravery, spontaneity, virility and proficiency. They responded with acclamation. It was amplified by the press, which hailed him as Galahad.

By the end of the war, which saw the collapse of the Romanov, Hohenzollern, Habsburg and Ottoman dynasties, the Prince of Wales seemed plainly ordained to safeguard the future of the house of Windsor. During the conflict he had performed his frustrating task well enough to win plaudits from the public and even commendations from the king. Shy, modest, sincere and sympathetic, he was inevitably dubbed Prince Charming. With his golden hair, azure eyes, fine features and slim figure he might indeed have stepped out of a fairy tale or a Hollywood romance. He had a magnetic attraction for men as well as women. The epicene Lord Esher, that quintessential courtier, described him as 'the sweetest thing in uniform in all the Armies'. Yet Esher also noticed something grave, sombre, wistful in his expression, a 'look of *Weltschmerz* in his eyes'.[23] Others observed not just the melancholy in his gaze but the anger. This clearly reflected a growing revulsion against his lot. After the penitentiary of youth he contemplated a life shackled to stale custom and outworn tradition. To be sure, the prince was in many respects as conservative as the king. But enforced conformity, compounded by the veneration accorded to the heir to the throne, had fostered in him a spirit of rebellion against the old ways and the old gang – which had, after all, presided over Armageddon. He found royal ceremonial hollow and repugnant, and he infuriated his father by calling it 'good propaganda'[24] and 'stunting'. He was certainly prepared to put on a public show, but he reserved his right to enjoy private pleasures. In 1919, with portentous emphasis, the prince swore to his adored mistress, Freda Dudley Ward, that were it not for her, 'I should shoot or drown myself, to escape from this – life which has become so so foul & sad & depressing & miserable for me!!'[25]

# 2
# Prince Imperial

After the war the prince's secret passion for Mrs Dudley Ward dominated an existence that was overtly dedicated to enhancing loyalty to the crown throughout the British Empire. She was not his first love. He had earlier fallen for a series of patrician ladies, Portia Cadogan, Marion Coke and Rosemary Leveson-Gower. These were intense but probably platonic affairs. Sex did, however, become a serious preoccupation after 1916, when two of his equerries, Lord Claud Hamilton and Piers 'Joey' Legh, arranged for him to lose his virginity with a prostitute in Amiens. This was a familiar rite of passage, but it so stimulated the prince's carnal appetite that, he said, 'I don't think of anything but women now.'[1] Whenever possible in the following years, he took advantage of his position to indulge in fleeting liaisons with 'bits' and 'whizzbangs', to use his own terms, whom he deemed very common or quite revolting. Often these relationships were highly imprudent. In 1917 he wrote letters to a Parisian cocotte with whom he had a fling, enabling her to blackmail him. Later that year he was reported to be consorting with 'a certain German woman'.[2] In 1918 his misbehaviour with British nurses in Rome almost caused Lord Claud to resign from his service.

Accepting a rebuke, Edward promised to reform. But he remained a serial womanizer, even maintaining that promiscuity was good for his health. He told Freda Dudley Ward that little amusements 'don't matter a damn where love is concerned, & now I only call it "medicine" '.

She tactfully agreed and it is true that his love for her totally eclipsed his passing fancies. The letters he sent her, woefully illiterate but enlivened with underlinings and exclamation marks, were exercises in ecstasy:

> you'll always know that your poor sad worn-out little David so so entirely faithful & devoted to his precious sacred blessed divine little goddess & idol his Fredie whom he loves & adores & worships as no man has ever loved adored or worshipped before or ever will again!!

The glut of devotion was matched by a surfeit of abasement. The prince described himself as a worm, unworthy of her love. He was a selfish brute and could only grovel at her feet. He wanted her to be really foul to him, to curse and be cruel. Frequently he referred to her as 'mummie' and said that he needed a mother figure to dominate him. 'Christ how I wish you were here to scold me angel & how I do miss being kept in order.' Sometimes he reverted to baby talk: ' "Pleath" oh! "pleath" come back to your devoted & adoring petit amoureux.'[3] The psyche has its reasons which reason may not know, so inferences from these epistolary outpourings, which exactly prefigured those later addressed to Wallis Simpson, must be tentative. Still, it is probably fair to say that the prince was a case of arrested development and that he was prone to depression and masochism. He was not only mentally immature, telling Freda schoolboyish dirty jokes and admitting that he had not grown up, but physically callow. According to one aide he had 'absolutely no hair on his body'[4] and he may have suffered from hormonal problems as a result of a pubescent attack of mumps. Furthermore, as she later acknowledged, he '*liked* being humbled'.[5] His craving for a maternal figure whom he could love with infantile abandon must surely have been a reaction against the frigid domestic circumstances of his youth. Although Edward acquired a separate establishment (at York House, a wing of St James's Palace), he had to spend Christmas 1919 with his parents, and in a letter to Freda he gave his address as 'York Cottage (F – ck it!!!!)'.

Freda Dudley Ward was undoubtedly good for the Prince of Wales. An attractive, charming and sympathetic woman of his own age, born into a wealthy textile-manufacturing clan and married to a Liberal MP, she brought him the thrill of romance with a taste of family happiness. He became fond of Freda's two daughters and under her influence he moderated his drinking, smoking and swearing. He poured out his heart to her, at times inadvertently revealing an astonishing heartlessness. Stationed in Germany shortly after the armistice, he expressed to her standard feelings of hatred for the Huns while nurturing the less usual ambition to wipe them off the face of the earth. When his handicapped youngest brother John died in 1919, Edward told her that it was the greatest possible relief but complained that the court was plunged into mourning for him 'just as the war is over which cuts parties etc. right out!!'. Admitting to Freda that he was a terrible snob, Edward confessed that nothing irritated him more than genteel middle-class types. Even worse, though, was an indescribably coarse and revolting trade union leader to whom, the prince said, he almost had to cringe as a representative of the newly enfranchised masses. As the constraints and demands of his post-war role grew harder to bear, Edward's letters became a shrill litany of grievance. He was hopelessly imprisoned in Buckingham Palace; his crazily narrow-minded father was constantly thwarting and maddening him; the official side of his life was a sham; the days of kings and princes were past and 'monarchies are out-of-date though I know it's a rotten thing for me to say & sounds Bolshevik'.[6]

Actually the Prince of Wales was much perturbed by the Bolsheviks. They had not only murdered his Romanov relations – Tsar Nicholas II was King George V's lookalike cousin – but they threatened to undermine the British monarchy and to subvert the empire. Like the French Jacobins, the Russian communists spearheaded a revolution that crossed national boundaries. As well as causing upheavals in continental Europe, it lapped at the shores of England, where the Labour Party was in the ascendant and one trade union leader told a post-war rally that he hoped to see 'the Red Flag flying over Buckingham Palace'.[7] Inspired not only by Lenin but by President Woodrow Wilson, who had championed the principle of self-determination in his Fourteen Points, colonized races agitated for independence. But the peace settlement actually increased the size of the British Empire, in the shape of mandates over former enemy territories such as Mesopotamia, Palestine and Tanganyika. The enlarged edifice was more impressive but less stable. Ireland was racked by troubles. Gandhi led a campaign of civil disobedience in India. There were conflicts with Arab nationalists throughout the Middle East. In South Africa many Boers yearned to establish a republican free state. Even the 'white' Dominions of Canada, Australia and New Zealand, their loyalty burnished but their nationhood forged in war, wanted complete autonomy within the Commonwealth. Like the king himself, Prince Edward was apprehensive about the dangers facing crown and empire. In a letter to his father written on 5 November 1918 he warned that the 'epidemic of revolutions' would make life much harder for the remaining monarchies. Britain's was by far the strongest, but it could only remain so if royalty 'kept in the closest possible touch with the people'.

The prince promised to do his part and his first provincial tour of Britain, in the early summer of 1919, was specifically designed to counter the communist threat. He at once demonstrated a real flair for public relations. Edward had a genuine, if somewhat woolly, sympathy for the poor and the dispossessed. He cared especially about ex-servicemen and took a particular interest in housing conditions. Moreover he learned to communicate his concerns in excellent impromptu speeches. Where royalty had previously smiled and waved *de haut en bas*, Edward stepped down from his pedestal. He mixed freely, talked informally and shook myriad hands, a gesture he described as pump-handling. As a result he won golden opinions everywhere – save in Buckingham Palace. Here he was accused of eroding the mystery of monarchy, thus violating Walter Bagehot's oft-cited maxim that daylight should not be let in upon magic. How far modern kings and princes should unbend is a moot point, but Edward was probably right to think that they could not afford to be too aloof in a democratic age. Later in the year his technique certainly proved effective during his progress through Canada where, he told King George, it was vital to avoid condescension and pomposity. The first of his overseas tours, a series devised by Lloyd George to augment imperial harmony and assuage colonial discord, was a triumph. Criss-crossing the great Dominion, the prince was greeted with hysterical enthusiasm and performed with terrific élan. He was frequently mobbed. People bombarded him with flowers and, when he visited New York, with tickertape. They tore at his clothes. His right hand became so bruised with pump-handling that he had to use his left. While applauding his success, the king deplored these unseemly manifestations. The prince replied that the crowds 'just go mad & one is powerless!!'.[8]

Actually he was exhilarated by starring in what he regarded as a first-class carnival or a painted circus. The acclaim boosted his self-confidence, the obverse of a gnawing self-doubt. It also made him more impatient with the official elements of the show – ceremonies, receptions, inspections, addresses, banquets, balls. Such rigmarole he regarded as stuffy, artificial, a complete waste of time; and he dismissed his participation in it as 'princing' (later 'kinging'). Nor would he focus on diplomatic matters. His political adviser Edward Grigg, the ablest member of his entourage, found him maddening. He could not get his royal master to read anything, not even half a sheet of paper. Instead the prince devoted much of his considerable energy to shooting, fishing and golfing. He also exhausted himself by keeping late hours in nubile company. Back home at the end of 1919, he was blissfully reunited with Freda. But the imminence of another separation, this time on a five-month tour of the Antipodes, and the growing conviction that his public duties were inescapable, intolerable and futile, precipitated an especially acute bout of despondency. He unburdened himself to his private secretary, Godfrey Thomas:

> Christ how I loathe my job now and all the press 'puffed' empty 'succès'. I feel I'm through with it and long to die. For God's sake don't breathe a word of this to a *soul*. No one else must know how I feel about my life and everything . . . You probably think from this that I ought to be in the mad-house already . . . I do feel such a bloody little shit.[9]

Thomas told Edward to pull himself together. And Lloyd George insisted that he should be guided by the serious-minded Grigg, adding this fateful admonition: 'If you are one day to be a constitutional King, you must first be a constitutional Prince of Wales.'[10]

As a counterweight the prince included in his retinue a nineteen-year-old naval officer, Louis 'Dickie' Mountbatten, whose task was to cheer him up down under. He was

Edward's cousin as well as his confidant and his unofficial diary of the tour was relentlessly facetious. It recorded every kind of royal horseplay, from leapfrog on the quarterdeck of the battlecruiser *Renown* en route for New Zealand, to 'follow my leader' at a dance near Sydney, where everybody crawled under beds, squeezed through windows, pelted each other with wet sponges and did 'quite the maddest things imaginable'.[11] The prince flung himself into other recreations: cattle drives and point-to-points, which he enjoyed, and kangaroo hunts, which he thought a mouldy form of sport. He was quick to don fancy dress and at one of the jazz parties given for him he played the castanets. But his public engagements were arduous. Once again he was greeted with rapture. He seemed not so much a man as a talisman (or *mana*, to use the Maori term, the embodiment of sacred power). Crowds fought to touch the hem of his garments, to get a psychic charge from fingering his flesh. Politicians endeavoured to bask in his reflected glory. His schedule was impossibly packed, he was often late and nearly always dog-tired. To his chagrin he was obliged to consort with dignitaries rather than Diggers. Still worse were what he called native stunts, since he regarded Aboriginal people as diseased, verminous and monkey-like, 'the most revolting form of living creatures I've ever seen'.[12] The prince succumbed to moods of ill-temper, morosity and capriciousness. He told Mountbatten that he'd give anything to change places with him. Towards the end Edward teetered on the brink of a nervous breakdown, wondering if he would crack like an egg. But the public saw the polished facade, not the

unhappy prince, and he was saluted as the empire's greatest ambassador. He also won praise for coolness when
his train overturned on one leg of the journey. Edward
emerged from the wreckage clutching a cocktail shaker,
emblem of post-war hedonism.

At home for a year after his return in October 1920, the
prince was hell-bent on pleasure. Indeed, he and his brothers set the tone for the 'gay 'twenties' as a whole when, as
Bertie's wife Elizabeth later said, 'we did night club life
madly'.[13] After parties, dinners, dances and other entertainments, Edward and Freda liked to spend the small
hours at Mayfair's Embassy Club, all red plush and gilt
mirrors, where he was thought caddish for wearing a dinner jacket instead of the regulation white tie and tails. His
days were devoted to more strenuous and dangerous pur-
suits, mainly hunting and steeplechasing – he relished the
thrills and didn't mind the spills, some of which caused
injuries. The king remonstrated with him and his son
responded sharply, determined to indulge his own fancies
and keep his 'princing' duties within bounds. He wriggled
out of official functions when he could. Typically, he protested about having to broadcast to Boy Scouts at 9 p.m.
'as it bitches one's evening'.[14] A 'reluctant philanthropist',[15]
he was also apt to rebuff appeals from charities, though
some good causes benefited greatly from his patronage,
which added lustre to the royal aura. The prince did, in
fact, take a keen interest in money. He was slow to improve
housing conditions on his Kennington estate but quick to
secure secret tax exemptions for the Duchy of Cornwall
(pleading that his more active role in public affairs had

increased expenditure), which enabled him to 'accumulate an immense private fortune'.[16] Naturally he avoided a gratuitous show of extravagance, which might have alienated the masses. In any case he disliked plutocratic ostentation, especially as personified by the princes of India, his next imperial destination.

Here he was paraded like a fetish in the expectation that this would impress 'the Oriental mind'.[17] However in the wake of repressive measures culminating in the Amritsar massacre of 1919, Gandhi had proclaimed a boycott of the prince's tour. It proved quite effective and frustrated any hope he had of winning allegiance through personal contact. In fact the prince was hardly cut out for this role since he believed in the smack of white government and had little liking for the natives – when told that he was the reincarnation of the Emperor Akbar, he was 'not over-pleased at the idea of having been a "black man"'.[18] But he felt stifled by the tight security and by protocol so strict as to make the court at Windsor seem relaxed; and he caused offence by banging the drums and beating the cymbals at a dance in Lucknow, and sitting at table beside pretty ingénues rather than kippered memsahibs of suitable seniority.

He was also disenchanted with the princely states where he spent half his time in the subcontinent. The maharajas were, as his father told him, loyal to the imperial crown. But Edward had no taste for their baroque obeisance, let alone for marble palaces, gold thrones, jewelled howdahs and profligate tiger hunts – the shoot in Nepal cost an estimated £300,000 (some £13 million today). He disappointed the maharajas by preferring polo, horse-racing, pig-sticking and killing small game. Although he did contribute to his party's Indian bag of thirty tigers and nine rhinoceroses, he came to favour the ciné-camera as much as the rifle, pioneering a royal concern for conservation that combines uneasily with a fondness for blood sports. Nevertheless, for all the difficulties and disappointments of Edward's eastern tour, which took in Japan as well as Burma, Ceylon and Hong Kong, it enhanced his immense popularity at home. On his return in June 1922 he was hailed as the darling of the empire. In the words of the Reuters correspondent who reported on the prince's Indian odyssey, 'his personal magnetism had fairly captured the hearts of the populace'.[19]

The prince strengthened his ties with Canada on two private visits in 1923 and 1924, ostensibly to inspect the ranch he had earlier bought in Alberta, actually to sample the fleshpots of the New World. As usual he was delightful and rebarbative by turns. In fact he seemed to veer between the polar influences of two of his new retainers: Sir Alan 'Tommy' Lascelles, a pillar of English rectitude; and Captain Edward 'Fruity' Metcalfe, a convivial Irish roué. Lascelles initially thought the prince the most attractive man he'd ever met and a wonderful travelling companion. But he became increasingly disillusioned, saying that he felt like an actor-manager 'whose Hamlet persists in interrupting the play by balancing the furniture on the end of his nose'.[20] Addicted to smoking, drinking and womanizing, Metcalfe encouraged Edward's waywardness, which affronted his hosts and prompted flaring headlines in the

North American press. Promising Lascelles that he would reform while following Metcalfe's example, the prince was impressionable as well as intractable: although royally dogmatic, he was said to 'reset his watch by every clock he passed'.[21] Thus one of the most admired items at the British Empire Exhibition at Wembley in 1924, a life-sized statue of the Prince of Wales on his ranch carved out of 3,000 lbs of refrigerated Canadian butter, was a peculiarly appropriate symbol. It celebrated his firm attachment to the great transatlantic Dominion and his role as heir to a crown which was the golden bond of Commonwealth union. But his image was artificially sustained and it would melt in the heat of passion.

Still, the Prince of Wales showed how brilliantly he could present himself in the last of his Dominion tours, to South Africa (via the Gold Coast and Nigeria) in 1925. Here memories of the Boer War were still green and the new prime minister, General Hertzog, leader of the National Party, seemed to threaten secession from the empire. Speaking in Cape Town the prince made an eloquent plea that all should work together as one, which was especially effective for containing a few sentences in Afrikaans – Hertzog had championed the cause of linguistic parity. Edward visited the Bloemfontein memorial to the 27,000 Boer women and children who had died in British concentration camps. In small dorps scattered across the veldt he tried to achieve racial reconciliation – with Afrikaners, not with Africans. He even serenaded journalists on his ukulele, despite considering them virulent scum. Moreover he gave them no opportunity for gossip-mongering since there was nothing on his gruelling 10,000-mile journey, which took in Rhodesia, to lead him astray: the evening entertainments were dreary and he met only 'zeppelin-shaped women'. Throughout, according to Joey Legh, the prince was 'absolutely marvellous'.[22] He could not eradicate animosities between the two white tribes of South Africa. Arguably, however, he made it easier for Hertzog to subscribe to the 1926 Balfour Definition, whereby the Dominions were said to be 'autonomous communities within the British Empire'.[23] Five years later this declaration of virtual independence was enshrined in law by the Statute of Westminster and for another three decades South Africa glinted in the royal diadem.

The final stage of the prince's tour, a visit to South America to drum up trade, was less successful. Greeted with pomp and euphoria, he was jaded, erratic and inconsiderate, prompting criticism in Argentine newspapers. At home this behaviour pattern continued. Edward seldom rose before mid-morning. Admitting that he was not clever and knew nothing about anything, he was easily distracted and unable to concentrate on business. In carrying out his official functions he was increasingly unpunctual and unreliable, prone to cancel his attendance at short notice, sometimes sulky when he did appear. It is true that he identified himself with the poor and unemployed on visits to distressed areas. Believing that his main task was to allay disaffection in the interests of both national solidarity and the Windsor dynasty, he conducted these visits with energy as well as empathy. Indeed it might be said that, like his grandfather as described by Margot Asquith, the prince devoted what time he did not spend on pleasure and sport ungrudgingly to duty. However, like Oscar Wilde he could resist everything except temptation, and much was vouchsafed to him.

King George grew ever more worried by the playboy antics of his eldest son. Writing to Queen Mary he deplored reports that David danced 'every night & most of the night too' and he feared that 'people who don't know him will begin to think that he is either mad or the biggest rake in Europe'.[24] Actually almost all the publicity the prince attracted – and he was a media megastar *avant la lettre* – enhanced his glamour as the most eligible bachelor on earth. In the modish milieu of nightclubs, cocktails, lipstick, jazz, short skirts, bobbed hair, painted fingernails, the Charleston, the Black Bottom, the tango, rumba and maxixe, Edward was the cynosure of his own cult. Its anthem was the hit song, 'I've danced with a man, who's danced with a girl, who's danced with the Prince of Wales.'

The prince's indiscretions were not confined to social life. When the General Strike took place in 1926 King George, who privately urged the government to arrest some of its leaders, prudently insisted that his family should keep a low profile. According to Mountbatten, the king's letters to the prince were like those of 'a Director to his Assistant Manager',[25] and Edward ignored the injunction. He supported the Miners' Relief Fund and contributed £10 to it himself. But he also instructed his chauffeur to distribute copies of Winston Churchill's inflammatory newspaper the *British Gazette* and he himself drove around London with officers in the Metropolitan Police.

The prince admired the steadfast yet emollient way in which Stanley Baldwin defeated the strikers. But when the prime minister accompanied Edward to Canada in 1927 for celebrations of the Diamond Jubilee of the Confederation, he witnessed his irresponsibility at first hand. Lascelles was driven to the point of resignation by it and at a 'secret colloquy' with Baldwin in Ottawa he said bluntly that

> the Heir Apparent, in his unbridled pursuit of wine and women, and whatever selfish whim occupied him at the moment, was rapidly going to the devil, and unless he mended his ways, would soon become no fit wearer of the British Crown.

Surprisingly, since he liked Edward personally, Baldwin agreed. And when Lascelles said that he sometimes thought it would be the best thing for the country if the prince broke his neck in a point-to-point, Baldwin replied: 'God forgive me, I have often thought the same.'[26]

For Lascelles the last straw was the prince's conduct on his safari through Kenya in 1928. Here the white settler community was notorious for loose living, the epicentre of decadence being Nairobi's Muthaiga Club where the prince was offered cocaine and had sex thrust upon him. His most scandalous escapade followed from 'dallying with a certain blonde of easy virtue'.[27] He thus arrived late at a Government House cocktail party, retired early, got caught sliding down a drainpipe by an alert *askari* and eventually arrived at the Muthaiga Club accompanied by Beryl Markham, a lithe horse trainer with whom he was conducting a simultaneous affair, to be showered with bread rolls, pulled from his chair and rolled on the floor by the jealous Lady Delamere. The governor and his wife, who sometimes found the prince 'rather marvellous',[28] were exasperated by such lapses. But Lascelles was relatively tolerant. He was not even much put out when Edward endangered their lives in the bush by debating which of them was to shoot a charging elephant. However, he became incensed by the prince's response to cables from Baldwin urging him to come home because the king was seriously ill. Edward dismissed the summons as an election ploy and when Lascelles remonstrated with him he simply went off to complete the seduction of the wife of a district commissioner. However the prince did return to England, at high speed, galvanized by the prospect of inheriting what his sister-in-law Elizabeth would call 'the intolerable honour'[29] of kingship. George V recovered and Lascelles resigned, telling Edward that if he did not change his ways he would lose the throne. The prince thanked him for the lecture and remarked forlornly, 'I suppose the fact of the matter is that I'm quite the wrong person to be Prince of Wales.'[30]

# 3
# Public Figure, Private Life

The biographer of King Edward VIII is under more than usual temptation to read the life of his subject backwards, to see its end in its beginning, to assume that the Prince of Wales was doomed to become the Duke of Windsor. The premonitory signs look as clear to us in retrospect as they did at the time to insiders – courtiers, ministers, patricians. King George himself, who was full of gloomy forebodings about the succession, had warned his eldest son that his double life would be found out and that the public would recoil from him. And Edward too occasionally feared that the British people would get a nasty shock if they learned the truth about 'their press-made national hero'.[1] Far from printing exposés, however, the press continued to burnish his panoply and hymn his golden future. Always respectful and often obsequious, it transmuted princely platitudes into pearls of wisdom, published photographs (sometimes doctored) that invariably showed him in a good light, and transformed him into a creature of myth and fantasy for the delectation of the masses. As the deputy secretary to the Cabinet Tom Jones observed, newspapers invested royal personages with qualities they did not possess to create an illusion in the service of the state. Indeed the press was one of several agencies aiming to sustain a sacrosanct monarchy as the focus of patriotic loyalty in a world turned upside down by powerful new forces. Edward's fate was bound up in this larger struggle.

The popular press, which marked a revolution in the nation's reading habits, was about the same age as the Prince of Wales himself. Its birth may be said to have occurred in 1896 when Alfred Harmsworth, later Lord Northcliffe, launched the *Daily Mail*. Costing a halfpenny, exploiting novel technology such as telephones, typewriters and linotype machines, filled with advertisements for cheap consumer goods, swiftly distributed by train and soon by motor vehicle, and appealing to the newly educated and enfranchised lower-middle class, the *Mail* was an instant success. Other national newspapers followed in its wake, notably the *Daily Express* and the *Daily Mirror*. Collectively known as the Beefeater press, they were imbued with the belief that royal blue blood was good for the circulation. Whereas the old provincial mercuries had tended to be radical and nonconformist, the freshly minted products of Fleet Street favoured monarchism, conservatism and even jingoism. Editors seeking news and views attractive to a broad readership trumpeted the national throne and the imperial crown. The *Mail* said that it was fitting for Queen Victoria to pay homage to God at St Paul's Cathedral on her Diamond Jubilee since He alone was more majestic than she. In the same vein Northcliffe gave blanket coverage to other royal events, especially births, marriages and deaths. Holding that the power of the press was not so great as the power of suppress, he also wrote to Edward VII's private secretary asking for hints about 'what not to publish'.[2] The fourth estate might profess to live by disclosure, but where the sovereign was concerned it lived by discretion. George V's eldest son was the prime beneficiary of its reticence, though this did not diminish his fatal hostility to journalists. At the beginning of the abdication crisis the socialite MP Henry 'Chips' Channon noted in his diary that Edward was 'at his worst with Fleet Street, off-hand, angry and ungracious; he never treats them in the right way, or realizes that his popularity largely depends on them'.[3]

As Prince of Wales his popularity was also boosted by two further mass media of communication, radio and cinema newsreels. The BBC quickly became the megaphone of monarchy, presenting royal occasions, among them Edward's imperial tours, as a series of aural pageants. The sovereign's Christmas message, first broadcast in 1932, was still more inspiring and a couple of days before George V's death Baldwin agreed with the Corporation's Director-General, Sir John Reith, that 'kingship never stood higher in this country and that broadcasting had a lot to do with this'.[4] So did the newsreel companies, such as Pathé and Gaumont, which made the peripatetic prince an idol of the silver screen. Their treatment of him and his ilk was, as a recent historian says, 'uniformly deferential, respectful and supportive'.[5] Such regard, echoed whenever royalty figured in public (and often in private) discourse, was not just an expression of reverence for the cult of majesty. It also expressed a belief, by no means confined to the upper and middle classes, that the crown had a practical function as the cornerstone of the state as well as the apex of society. It had stood for order when Edwardian Britain faced threats from strikers, Suffragettes and Irishmen. It had epitomized the nation during the First World War. It was the *clou* of empire. To an untried democracy challenged by communism and fascism while afflicted by unemployment and depression, it offered historical continuity and political stability. Little wonder, then, that the Prince of Wales was cast as a demigod. This was an uneasy role for one so averse to humbug, yet he took immunity to criticism as his due, failing to realize that the ultimate price of privilege was duty.

Of course Edward was by no means deaf to the call of duty. During his father's illness he responded to his mother's plea to give up steeplechasing by selling his horses and concentrating on the less hazardous sport of golf, though he did resume flying for a time. He also earned his parents' gratitude by helping to rescue his brother George, Duke of Kent, from a slough of drugs and dissipation. He took George on another tour to promote trade in South America where, admittedly, he did not always set him a good example. And in due course the delinquent duke was safely married off to the lovely Princess Marina of Greece – during their Greek Orthodox wedding ceremony the Prince of Wales unthinkingly lit a cigarette from a priestly candle.

As the economic blizzard raged after the 1929 slump, Edward made more visits to areas of industrial stagnation, where he was often greeted with mute apathy. He had no solution to the country's problems but prided himself on his social conscience, conveyed fellow feeling for the jobless and initiated one or two modest ameliorative efforts. The best-known was the Feathers Clubs Association, which raised funds for youth projects. It was headed by Freda Dudley Ward, to whom Edward was still devoted. This did not inhibit him from acquiring a new *maîtresse en titre*, Thelma Lady Furness, the camellia-skinned half-American wife of a shipping magnate. In her autobiographical account, which is not necessarily incredible despite being written in the style of Barbara Cartland, she records that they consummated their affair when he returned to Africa in 1930 to complete his safari: 'His arms about me were the only reality; his words of love my only bridge to life. Borne along on the mounting tide of his ardour, I felt myself being inexorably swept from the accustomed moorings of caution.'[6]

Thelma Furness became a regular visitor to Fort Belvedere, the grace and favour residence on the edge of Windsor Great Park which Edward acquired from his father later in 1930 and which became the new delight of his life. Built as a royal folly in the eighteenth century and later picturesquely embellished by the Regency architect Sir Jeffry Wyatville, the Fort was a mock-Gothic mélange of towers, turrets and battlements. Edward renovated it, installing modern conveniences such as central heating and en suite bathrooms. He added a tennis court and a swimming pool. And with frenetic zeal he took a personal part in clearing and replanting the grounds, recruiting often reluctant guests as assistant gardeners. The Fort provided, as King George had surmised, a private retreat for the prince's weekend entertaining. Its keynote was louche frivolity in the manner of contemporary bright young things, among whom Lady Furness was a leading light. Edward called her Toodles; she called him the Little Man. She petted him, danced with him, taught him to embroider, played him at backgammon, exchanged teddy bears with him and encouraged him in displays of irresponsibility. In Africa one of these had taken the form of betting the hunter Denys Finch Hatton that he could not affix a picture of King George to the hindquarters of a rhinoceros – a bet he won by sticking two postage stamps on the animal while it dozed. At the Fort, Lady Furness recalled, Edward engaged in rowdy pranks such as vying with his brother Bertie to see whether gramophone records really were, as their labels said, unbreakable. Together the princes threw them around like discuses and boomerangs, making guests duck and dodge amid howls of laughter and finally knocking over a valuable lamp.

More serious were the prince's political *faux pas*, particularly in relation to Nazi Germany. During the war, of course, he had loathed the Huns, among them his own relations, formally disowned when his father changed the family name to Windsor. But like many others, including his mother who now reckoned that Britain had backed the wrong horse in 1914, Edward soon came to favour Germany. He saw it as the victim of a punitive peace, as a bulwark against communism (in France as well as Russia) and, after 1933, as a model of how a progressive dictatorship could defeat the scourge of unemployment. Despite Hitler's mouthing aggression, murdering rivals and mounting an ever more vicious campaign against Jews, Edward made no secret of his sympathy with the Third Reich. According to its ambassador Leopold von Hoesch, he criticized the Foreign Office for being too one-sided in its attitudes, professed unconcern about German rearmament and advocated the renascence of the Reich in terms that corresponded 'word for word with the opinion of our Führer'.[7]

As well as approving of Oswald Mosley and supporting Mussolini's assault on Ethiopia, Edward stoked gossip about his totalitarian leanings by publicly endorsing the British Legion's proposal to send a goodwill mission to Germany. His father reproached him for meddling in matters of party controversy, but Edward felt justified in intervening when he thought national security was at stake. Ironically the king was, if possible, even more horrified by the prospect of another war than the prince. But George V knew that the monarchy's survival depended on maintaining its constitutional neutrality, whereas his successor would soon convince well-informed observers such as Chips Channon that he 'is going the dictator way, and is pro-German'.[8] It is true that Edward was deeply tainted by anti-Semitism and wanted to attend the Berlin Olympic Games. Yet he was a follower of fashion rather than an incipient autocrat. He viewed the new creed as simply the latest in political chic. It was not a matter of jackboots and rubber truncheons but of swastika cufflinks and tailored black shirts, the appurtenances of what one newspaper called 'Savile Row Fascism'.[9]

Stylishness was what chiefly appealed to Edward about the *femme fatale* who revolutionized his life in 1934. She was Mrs Ernest Simpson, described by one of the prince's admirers as 'a woman clear-cut as a gem'.[10] Born Bessie Wallis Warfield in Pennsylvania in 1896, she always took pride in coming from old Southern stock. But her tubercular father died when she was a baby and her mother Alice, *née* Montague, had to rely on the charity of rich relations. Wallis, as she required to be called, was sent to a genteel Baltimore boarding school and launched into Society. Svelte and vivacious, with a strong jaw and expressive violet eyes, she attracted many suitors and acquired a reputation for being fast. Certainly she married quickly, aged just nineteen. Her husband, a naval officer called Earl Winfield Spencer, turned out to be a drunken bully. They separated but in 1924, after an abortive affair with an Argentine diplomat, she followed her husband to a new posting in China. Here his alcoholism worsened and, Wallis wrote in her memoirs, he made her accompany him to Hong Kong sing-song houses 'where he would ostentatiously make a fuss over the girls'.[11]

Such behaviour not only precipitated their divorce but fuelled persistent rumours that she had picked up arcane sexual techniques in the Orient with which she held the Prince of Wales in thrall. There is no evidence for this or for other lurid stories about her past. But as a lone female of slender means she did have an adventurous time amid the sybaritic expatriate community in China and was said to be 'infamous for arousing bouts of passion among adoring males'.[12] One she beguiled on her return to the United States was Ernest Simpson, a half-English shipping broker whose own marriage was on the rocks. He was cultivated but conventional and they had little in common. However, as Wallis told her mother when announcing her intention to wed him in 1928, she was fond of Ernest and he was kind. He offered her a secure, comfortable base in London and at the age of thirty-two she said, 'I really feel so tired of fighting the world all alone and with no money.'[13] She may also have felt that his dullness would accentuate her sparkle.

Homesick in the foggy metropolis, troubled by an ulcer and anguished by the death of her mother, Wallis did not shine at first. But in 1929 she and Ernest established themselves in a flat near Marble Arch that was spacious and modish by middle-class standards, though the opulent Channon would dismiss it as dreadful and banal. It was staffed by four servants, from whom Wallis demanded the highest standards on pain of instant dismissal, and it enabled her to entertain with some success. She led an active social life, playing bridge, attending parties and meeting many Americans engaged in business and diplomacy. One of them was related to Thelma Furness, through whom the Simpsons were introduced to the Prince of Wales at Melton Mowbray, the Mecca of fox-hunting, in 1931. Despite spending a whole day on her hair and nails, Wallis initially made little impression on him. Although dashing and diverting, she was less smart and sophisticated than she later became. On first acquaintance, indeed, she struck the Society photographer Cecil Beaton as raucous and appalling, a brawny bullock in Sapphic blue velvet: 'I thought her awful, common, vulgar, strident, a second-rate American with no charm.'[14] Such supercilious verdicts were commonplace and it is true that Wallis had no claims to be considered beautiful, let alone voluptuous. Her hair was too straight, her mouth too hard and her chin too square. She had mannish hands, a mole on her face and her figure was as angular as a diamond chiselled by Cartier. But it was precisely her edgy, adamantine quality that soon began to attract the Prince of Wales. He was fascinated by her steely self-assurance, her brittle wit and her art deco sheen. She was a model of what the wealthy Conservative MP Ronald Tree called 'metallic elegance'.[15]

Certainly Wallis was tough: another parliamentarian, Duff Cooper, said she was 'as hard as nails and she doesn't love him'.[16] But she appreciated that the prince himself was, in the words of a third Tory politician, R. A. Butler, 'congenitally weak'.[17] As a practised vamp she recognized that he yearned to subsume himself into a stronger personality, that he craved not so much a mistress as a master. Lacking the native awe for royalty, Wallis transfixed him with a fearless gaze and talked to him with a naturalness that initially astonished and subsequently captivated him. By 1933 the Simpsons were regular guests at Fort Belvedere and Edward often visited their flat, where he once played the bagpipes, stood on his head and stayed until three o'clock in the morning. Rumours swirled around them. Writing to her beloved aunt Mrs Bessie Merryman, Wallis dismissed them as gossip, described herself as the prince's 'comedy relief' and said that 'I always have Ernest hanging around my neck so all is safe.' Moreover, she added primly, 'I'm not in the habit of taking my girlfriends' beaux.'[18] However that was exactly what she did when

Thelma Furness, entrusting the Little Man to her care, went to America early in 1934, where she engaged in a brief dalliance with the Aly Khan. On her return she noticed that Wallis and Edward were sharing private jokes and that when he picked up salad with his fingers she gave him a playful slap on the hand. In the late spring he brusquely excluded Thelma from his circle. And when Freda Dudley Ward telephoned she was told by the operator at York House that her calls could no longer be put through to the prince. It was a craven, callous and permanent dismissal.

The reason is plain: Edward was now becoming even more abjectly fixated on Wallis than he had been on Freda. He let her rule the roost at Fort Belvedere, where the staff resented their imperious new chatelaine. He dispensed the first drops in what became a cascade of jewellery. In the summer he took her on a continental holiday without Ernest, though chaperoned by her Aunt Bessie. From Biarritz they went on a cruise with the Guinness heir Lord Moyne. His yacht *Rosaura*, a converted Channel steamer, was no stranger to adultery; and off the Spanish coast, Wallis would coyly record, she and the prince 'crossed the line that marks the indefinable boundary between friendship and love'.[19] Whatever her amatory arts, she clearly exerted a potent psychological hold over him. On the Riviera she rationed his pleasures – drinking, dancing and staying up late. She criticized his clothes. Despite a constitutional restlessness, he waited two hours for her at a hairdresser's in Cannes. By the end of their travels, one of his equerries noted, the prince had 'lost all confidence in himself and follows W around like a dog'.[20] At home she hoped to conduct a harmonious *ménage à trois*, remaining securely with Ernest while enjoying the thrills and privileges of being the royal favourite. Having seen how Edward snuffed out old flames, she suspected that the position would be temporary and, acquisitive from her impecunious youth up, she plainly hoped to profit while it lasted. But Wallis reckoned without the overpowering infatuation she had inspired in the prince by her skill as a dominatrix.

Intent on marrying her, he tried to convince others that she was the acme of perfection. Nothing loth, Society hostesses such as Emerald Cunard and Sybil Colefax toadied to her shamelessly. But when the prince invited Wallis to a reception at Buckingham Palace the king was incensed. He banished her from royal occasions and took to raging about the caddishness of his eldest son. Several courtiers tried in vain to warn Edward about the dangers of his liaison, but he ignored them and pleaded with his father to lift the ban on Wallis, swearing she was not his mistress. This shocked those who had reason to know otherwise and King George was soon persuaded that his son had lied to him. Edward's enslavement to Mrs Simpson clouded the king's Silver Jubilee in 1935, an extended celebration which confirmed the immeasurable esteem in which the royal patriarch was held and provided a wholesome contrast to brutal exhibitions of power in Nuremberg and Moscow. Meanwhile the Prince of Wales was sublimely happy in the presence of his inamorata, taking her on further holidays, skiing in Kitzbühel, waltzing in Vienna, listening to Gypsy music in Budapest, and again yachting in the Mediterranean. Away from her, as Winston Churchill would observe, he was haggard and dejected. He sent her lavish gifts and pathetic letters: 'Oh! A boy does miss and want a girl here so terribly tonight.' She responded firmly, chiding him for being selfish and naïve: 'you haven't grown up where love is concerned and ... may always remain Peter Pan'.[21] Sometimes she mocked or scolded him so cruelly that he burst into tears. The prince seemed to revel in his humiliation. At one country house party he asked if Wallis had a light for his cigarette and she made him beg for it like a dog.

Protected by the reticence of his intimates, the deference of the media and the fidelity of the people, the Prince of Wales thought that he could behave as he liked in private. George V was convinced that Edward would injure the monarchy and hoped that he would abdicate in favour of his brother Bertie. Anxious about the future and worn out by the demands of the jubilee, the king went into a decline. On 16 January 1936 Queen Mary summoned her eldest son to Sandringham where, in the words of the famous medical bulletin, the king's life was slowly moving towards its close. The royal doctor assisted the process with an injection designed to ease his patient's passing and to ensure it was announced in respectable morning papers such as *The Times* rather than in 'the less appropriate evening journals'.[22] Perhaps for this reason, perhaps in sorrow for sustaining the perennial hostility between monarch and heir, perhaps because he mourned his princely youth and lamented his kingly state, Edward VIII, as he became shortly before midnight on 20 January, gave way to 'frantic and unreasonable' grief.[23]

Weeping uncontrollably, he clung to his mother who, with characteristic sangfroid, paid homage to him as her new sovereign. He also made the abrupt decision to scrap 'Sandringham time', which was half an hour ahead of Greenwich to give extra daylight for shooting: 'I'll fix those bloody clocks.'[24] He then broke with tradition by flying to London and watching his own proclamation as King-Emperor – from a window in St James's Palace, where in the background could be discerned the shadowy form of Mrs Simpson. On 23 January Edward marched with his brothers behind the gun carriage taking the body of their father from King's Cross station to lie in state at Westminster Hall. Amid a vast throng the new king still looked, at the age of forty-one, refreshingly young – he was variously said to have a boy's body, a valet's hands and a dentist's smile. But he seemed sad, lost and bewildered. As the cortège trundled into New Palace Yard the jewelled Maltese Cross on top of the imperial crown, which was resting on the coffin, shook loose and fell to the ground. It was retrieved by a Grenadier guardsman. Many thought the mishap a bad omen and King Edward was heard to say, 'Christ! What will happen next?'[25]

# 4
# King Edward's Reign

What happened next was an extraordinary outpouring of woe and hope. A million people shuffled past King George's catafalque and the new monarch made an inspired gesture by mounting a brief vigil over it with his brothers the night before the funeral. The multitudes flanking the procession next day were the largest London had seen, but even they were dwarfed by the radio audience for the service at St George's Chapel, Windsor. So emotional were the obsequies, noted the writer Philip Gibbs, that they generated a kind of mass hysteria. It was compounded by heightened expectations of King Edward VIII, whom Gibbs described as the 'most popular man in the world'.[1] His social concerns had been informed by arduous travels at home and abroad and it was often said that there never was a prince better prepared to ascend the throne of his ancestors. Winston Churchill offered the heartfelt wish that 'Your Majesty's name will shine in history as the bravest and best beloved of all the sovereigns who have worn the island Crown.'[2] And if the language was characteristically orotund, the prospect did not seem extravagant. The novelist Compton Mackenzie discerned in Edward 'the genius of royalty'.[3] The journalist Hannen Swaffer thought the new king fit to 'build a New World'.[4] The historian Philip Guedalla said that if there were no monarchy Edward 'would be the uncrowned king of England'.[5] As storm clouds gathered over Europe, most British subjects could anticipate a reign both happy and glorious.

However the tiny minority who knew about Edward's obsession with Mrs Simpson were less optimistic and even the *Daily Mail* struck a note of caution. Its chief leader writer penned a standard eulogy of kingship – freighted with high spiritual values, rich in indefinable associations, full of symbolic and mystical meaning, surrounded by pomp and circumstance – but he concluded that 'the true royalty of the Throne lies in the service which the King renders to his country'.[6] Courtiers and ministers worried from the start about how Edward would fulfil his duties. Initially he seemed bent on doing too much: he proposed not to accept Cabinet decisions blindly but to exercise his prerogatives more freely than his father had done. Indeed, Edward apparently told his Nazi cousin the Duke of Coburg that he was 'resolved to concentrate the business of government on himself'.[7] The king's style, too, would be different. While preserving essential traditions, he aimed to discard superfluous flummery and make the monarchy less remote from the people. He wanted 'to throw open the windows a little and to let into the venerable institution some of the fresh air that I had become accustomed to breathe as Prince of Wales'. He aspired, in short, to become 'Edward the Innovator'.[8] In his memoirs he wryly observed that his achievement had been limited to abolishing the rule that Yeomen of the Guard should wear spade beards and initiating the King's Flight, which provided him with a pilot and a twin-engine Dragon Rapide biplane. And he suggested that his failure to accomplish more was attributable to the rigidity of prevailing convention, which probably meant that a modern monarch was a contradiction in terms. However, as became obvious to Major Alexander Hardinge, who succeeded Lord Wigram as the king's private secretary in May 1936, Edward was so involved with Mrs Simpson that he was 'incapable of transacting the simplest official business'.[9]

This harsh verdict, although correct in essence, needs some qualification. Many who met Wallis Simpson, among them Tory MPs such as Victor Cazalet and Lady Astor, thought that she inspired Edward to do his best. The Surveyor of the King's Pictures, Kenneth Clark, said that she cheered him up and 'did him a ton of good'.[10] Duff Cooper was impressed that she stopped the king visiting her flat, and told him to use the largest royal Daimler so that his subjects could see him. Noting that Wallis forbade him to smoke during the *entr'acte* at the theatre, the diarist Harold Nicolson described her as 'bejewelled, eyebrow-plucked, virtuous and wise'.[11] Chips Channon liked and admired her as 'a woman of charm, sense, balance and great wit, with dignity and taste. She has always been an excellent influence on the King.'[12] It is true that the new monarch, who in some moods liked his job, had remarkably little grasp of what it entailed: Archbishop Cosmo Gordon Lang recorded him as saying that he understood he 'had now to appoint bishops and asked me to tell him how it was done!'.[13] But he began his reign with an impressive burst of zeal.

The king worked assiduously on the official papers in his red boxes. He carried out most of his ceremonial functions with affability and aplomb. He also streamlined some of them: debutantes were presented more informally, at garden parties, and loyal addresses were presented together instead of individually. Among other reforms, he ended the prime-ministerial custom of sending regular political reports to Buckingham Palace. As a memorial to his father, he championed the King George's Field Foundation for the provision of playing fields throughout the country. Like royalty everywhere, Edward laid down the law about decorations and dress, though his notions of sartorial propriety sometimes seemed dangerously avant-garde – he dispensed with the frock coat as an item of court apparel and did away with mourning caps, veils and crêpe. He concerned himself with other such trivia, insisting that the new design of stamps and coins should be changed to display his more photogenic left profile. However he did take a voluble and opinionated, if ineffective, interest in foreign affairs. When Hitler occupied the Rhineland in March 1936 the king sent a 'stinging rebuke'[14] to his brother-in-law Lord Harewood for protesting about it and he was said to be 'extraordinarily active'[15] in preventing an aggressive British response, itself hardly on the cards. Edward left the Italian ambassador in no doubt about his opposition to the League of Nations' sanctions on Italy, imposed in response to Mussolini's invasion of Ethiopia, and he refused the request of Foreign Secretary

Anthony Eden to meet the exiled Emperor Haile Selassie. He did, though, overcome his reluctance to shake hands with the Soviet commissar Maxim Litvinov, whom he first asked, 'Why did you kill my cousin?'[16] and then quizzed about 'the possibilities of big-game shooting in Russia'.[17]

As that fancy suggests, the king lacked the intellectual stamina to concentrate on serious matters for long, particularly since, as Stanley Baldwin observed, his infatuation with Mrs Simpson 'obliterated part of his mind'.[18] The surviving part was fixated on pleasing her, especially in money matters. Capable of open-handedness in youth, Edward had become tight-fisted with age and he now turned into a royal Scrooge. If this was mainly to satisfy Wallis's rapacity it was also an expression of his fury at having been left out of his father's will. As he heard its provisions, which allocated about £750,000 to each of his siblings, he kept repeating: 'Where do I come in?'[19] Lord Wigram explained that he ought to have amassed a large surplus – it actually amounted to about £1 million – from the Duchy of Cornwall and that he could save more, as the late king had, from the Civil List. Edward remained embittered and he initiated an economy drive which was not so much thrifty as mean. He sacked staff, among them faithful old retainers. He reduced wages and salaries, even cutting Alexander Hardinge's remuneration by 10 per cent, and abolished perquisites such as beer allowances. He also found ways of augmenting his income. The king transferred to himself nearly all the fund accumulated by the Duchy of Lancaster from the estates of those who died intestate, £37,000 or

£2.3 million at today's values. (Perhaps with abdication in mind, he also tried, unsuccessfully, to get his hands on £250,000 of the Duchy's capital.) And he induced the Air Ministry to pay for the King's Flight, which was sometimes used to import Paris fashions for Mrs Simpson, evading Customs duty, and to bring into the country, ignoring quarantine regulations, the Cairn terrier he had given her. Called Slipper, it was an adored bond between them, a substitute love child.

Consumed by his own affair, the king soon allowed affairs of state to pale into insignificance. He scarcely bothered to hide his weariness with the rituals of sovereignty and did everything to dodge them. Keeping irregular hours, he made visitors wait for long periods, among them Baldwin himself. To avoid the fogeyish Wigram, he once climbed out of a Buckingham Palace window, sloping off to see Mrs Simpson. Edward had begun by ticking official documents he read and returning them promptly; but the ticks became sparse and slow to appear, and they were sometimes superseded by rings made by wine glasses at Fort Belvedere. Finding work on his boxes drudgery and telling Wallis that state papers were mostly bunk, he eventually stopped reading them 'almost completely'.[20] Yet he was quite capable of handing them to her in full view of guests, and acclaiming her judgements 'with ecstatic admiration'.[21] Such breaches of security alarmed the government. Mrs Simpson supposedly had pro-Nazi sympathies and the king was putty in her hands. So ministers starved him of confidential information, tapped his telephone and kept him under surveillance. The Special Branch also spied on

Mrs Simpson herself, who told her Aunt Bessie how hard she was finding it 'to please, amuse, placate two men'.[22] According to police reports, however, she was also endeavouring to please a third man. He was Guy Marcus Trundle, a married car salesman described as a 'very charming adventurer', who had secret trysts with her where 'intimate relations take place'.[23]

This affair, if it existed outside the snoopers' heated imagination, was a bagatelle beside the king's matter. Edward's fixed purpose was matrimony and in one of his febrile love letters he insisted that '*no* difficulties or complications can possibly prevent our ultimate happiness ... God bless WE [i.e. Wallis and Edward] for ever'.[24] The obstacles were, indeed, formidable. One was Ernest Simpson himself, torn between the honour of laying down his wife for his king and the shame of being the butt of such jokes. Edward encouraged his complaisance, possibly by holding out the hope of an accolade, certainly by sponsoring his entry into an influential Masonic lodge – to the indignation of other members. To enable Wallis to obtain a divorce the king had to conceal his intentions, but early in his reign he made them crystal-clear to her husband, exclaiming rhetorically: 'Do you really think that I would be crowned without Wallis by my side?'[25] Simpson was willing, soon finding comfort in the arms of his wife's best friend; but Wallis herself remained uncertain and securing her compliance was not straightforward. Certainly she was seduced by the social power and, still more, the material wealth which Edward conferred. Not only did he settle some £250,000 on Wallis, he pandered to her 'love affair' with gems, which she played with 'like a child with toys'.[26] Some of the stones he gave her were so large that they resembled costume jewellery, while others were exquisitely cut and inscribed with amorous messages, such as 'WE are too [*sic*]'.[27] So in May 1936 Wallis informed her aunt that her marriage had collapsed and that she would take her chances with the king. But as late as mid September, nerve-racked by the imminence of her divorce, she told Edward that she must return to Ernest since 'you and I would only create disaster together'. According to Lascelles, the king threatened to slit his throat if she left him. At any rate he quashed her doubts, declaring that he loved her 'Madly tenderly adoringly'.[28]

As early as February 1936 Wigram had divined that Edward aimed to make Wallis his queen; but to almost everyone else who knew of their affair it was inconceivable that he could contemplate marrying a woman whom Hardinge characterized as a 'two-bit trollop'.[29] Although Mrs Simpson's name featured in the Court Circular, as far as ordinary British people were concerned there was scarcely a breath of impending scandal to tarnish the king's majesty. Indeed, on 16 July he won heartfelt plaudits for his unruffled response to an apparent assassination attempt – a man threw a pistol at him as he rode back to Buckingham Palace from a Colours ceremony in Hyde Park. Furthermore preparations for his crowning proceeded steadily. Processional arrangements were made, rituals were brushed up, dress codes were promulgated, festivities were planned and thousands of new Prayer Books were printed. Domestic manufacturers confidently produced masses of flags, favours, souvenirs, bunting and coloured lights, to say nothing of novelty items such as Union Jack shoes and some seven million coronation mugs. However the king's August cruise from the Adriatic to the Bosphorus on board Lady Yule's sumptuous steam yacht *Nahlin* alerted the rest of the world to his relationship with Mrs Simpson.

The voyage was a blaze of indiscretion from the start. Despite the danger of seeming to countenance Mussolini's intervention in the Spanish Civil War, Edward wanted to embark at Venice and he was intensely irritated by having, on Foreign Office advice, to set off from a less romantic Yugoslavian port. In the quest for pleasure he did not count the cost, converting the *Nahlin*'s library into a bedroom, driving thousands of golf balls into the sea for the fun of watching the splash, and resisting official engagements. In Istanbul he wished to play golf without seeing any dignitaries and only the British ambassador's threat of resignation induced him to meet Kemal Atatürk. No doubt this and other such reluctant encounters gained Britain a measure of diplomatic goodwill, but they were eclipsed by the king's undignified appearances elsewhere. He sailed shirtless through the Corinth Canal, dined in a disreputable Athens bistro, wandered naked around a Turkish bath in Vienna. Above all he was endlessly pictured with Wallis, sometimes in poses of revealing tenderness. Heedless of Anzac sensibilities, he even took her to Gallipoli. British newspapers loyally kept mum – the *Daily Telegraph* even omitted Mrs Simpson's name from the *Nahlin*'s guest list. But the continental and American press reported that the king made no attempt to hide his favourite from Balkan crowds, who shouted 'Zivila Ljubav' – 'Long Live Love'. Wallis herself was alarmed by these demonstrations, reproaching Edward for his lack of discretion. He replied that discretion was 'a quality which, though useful, I have never particularly admired'.[30]

Back home the king continued on his reckless course, which provoked the first stirrings of adverse publicity. He thought nothing of flagging down taxis for Mrs Simpson in St James's or painting her toenails beside the swimming pool at Fort Belvedere, which prompted a footman to give notice. Nor did he scruple to requisition pictures from the National Gallery to embellish Fort Belvedere. But Edward's worst mistake related to his refusal to open the new Aberdeen Infirmary on 23 September, giving the bogus excuse that the court was still in mourning for his father. On that very day, when the Duke of York was deputizing for him at the hospital, Edward, barely disguised in motoring goggles, drove sixty miles from Balmoral to pick up Mrs Simpson from Aberdeen railway station. The city's *Evening Express* juxtaposed photographs of the two events, to the clear detriment of the sovereign. Mrs Simpson then acted as hostess at the shrine of Victorian Balmorality. Guests such as the Duchess of York were horrified by her proprietorial airs – 'this tartan's gotta go'.[31] But the besotted monarch now kept his family at arm's length, intent only on ensuring that Wallis achieved a trouble-free divorce. Reporting on 16 October that the suit would be undefended, the *New York Journal* said that London Society was 'stunned by the possibility of an American Queen'.

Edward at once solicited Lord Beaverbrook's help to suppress news of the case in Britain, saying that Mrs Simpson was 'distressed by the thought of notoriety'.[32] Beaverbrook secured a 'gentlemen's agreement' with other press owners whereby nearly all journals censored themselves, a conspiracy of silence assisted by newsagents who literally cut out revelations from imported foreign publications. The *New York Times* was amazed by this 'voluntary surrender of the freedom of the press', a dangerous precedent that anyway defeated its own purpose 'by giving gossip-mongers unbridled liberties'.[33] This was an astute assessment, but the king was emboldened by the docility of Britain's fourth estate.

He remained uncooperative when Stanley Baldwin visited Fort Belvedere on 20 October. The prime minister had long feared that a crisis would be precipitated unless the king concealed his association with Mrs Simpson, as he would have done if 'she were what I call a respectable whore'.[34] But now, faced by Cabinet anxieties about the fate of the throne and requests for direction from the likes of Geoffrey Dawson, editor of the London *Times*, Baldwin could no longer take refuge in masterly inactivity. The meeting was fraught, Baldwin asking for a mid-morning whisky and Edward refusing to join him on the grounds that he never drank before seven o'clock. Spurning any hint that he might keep Mrs Simpson as a secret mistress, he also refused Baldwin's request that he should try to halt the divorce proceedings, which was solely a matter for her. So the case was swiftly concluded at the next available assizes, held on 27 October in Ipswich, where citizens were astonished by the attendance of so many foreign journalists and cameramen, whose activities were forcefully constrained by the police. Transatlantic newspapers proclaimed that the king would wed Mrs Simpson once the decree nisi became absolute. Outraged by the headlines, an expatriate signing himself Britannicus wrote a pertinent letter to *The Times*, which Dawson showed to Hardinge and Baldwin. While misrepresenting American opinion, which favoured a democratic monarchy under the auspices of Queen Wally, Britannicus confirmed their view that the king had transformed Britain 'from a sober and dignified realm into a dizzy Balkan musical comedy attuned to the rhythm of jazz'.[35]

Ironically, during his last weeks on the throne Edward performed his public duties with panache. At Buckingham Palace he presided over two diplomatic receptions with skill and confidence. On 3 November, although disappointing the crowds by arriving at Parliament in a closed Daimler rather than an open carriage, he played his part serenely at the State Opening, despite the overpowering smell of mothballs from the peers' robes. He lent gravity to the proceedings on Armistice Day. His inspection of the Home Fleet at Portland was, in the words of Sir Samuel Hoare, First Lord of the Admiralty, 'one long series of personal triumphs'.[36] Equally successful was his strenuous tour (18–19 November) of depressed areas in south Wales. Viewing squalid villages and derelict pits, the king was visibly moved by the plight of malnourished children and jobless miners. They cheered him to an echo and he famously gave them hope by saying, 'Something must be done . . . and I will do all I can to assist you.'[37] He meant well but his sympathy was skin-deep. He had already decided to abdicate and on his return to London he attended a magnificent dinner party at Chips Channon's Mayfair mansion, assuring his hostess that 'he approved of splendour'. Aware of the impending drama, Channon himself concluded: 'The King is insane about Wallis, insane.'[38] Some insiders thought him the victim of witchery or erotomania, but most, recalling the malady of George III, shared Channon's view. Baldwin, Archbishop Lang, Hardinge and others believed that Edward was mentally ill. Lascelles overheard Wigram saying to himself, 'He's mad – he's mad. We shall have to lock him up.'[39]

Behind the scenes events moved rapidly to a climax. On 13 November Hardinge brusquely warned the king that press silence would soon be broken, which might trigger a political crisis, and he urged that Mrs Simpson should leave the country. After taking counsel with his old friend Walter Monckton, Edward summoned Baldwin on 16 November and informed him that he intended to marry Mrs Simpson and that if necessary he would renounce the throne. That evening he confided in Queen Mary. She refused his request to meet Wallis, having promised her husband not to receive this 'adventuress'.[40] He answered maternal calls to duty and sacrifice by repeating, 'All that matters is our happiness.'[41] The following day Edward told his brother Bertie, who was shattered by the news, fearing that the whole monarchical edifice would crumble and that he, quite unsuited to the task, would have to pick up the pieces. With Baldwin's agreement the king then talked to friends in the government. They found him adamant for marriage and ready for departure. To Hoare he exclaimed, 'No single middle-aged man willingly stays in a tomb.'[42] To Duff Cooper's suggestion that he mask his wedding plans until after the coronation, Edward replied that he could not participate in this solemn ceremony without being frank with his subjects. Another friend, Esmond Harmsworth, whose father Lord Rothermere owned the *Daily Mail*, proposed a compromise – a morganatic marriage. Although finding this distasteful, since Wallis would be his consort but not his queen, the king asked Baldwin to consider it, evidently failing to realize that the resultant advice would be binding. The prime minister thought the alien expedient no more acceptable than having a twice-divorced American on the throne. Labour and Liberal chiefs, who reckoned that the nonconformist conscience, which was still powerful at home and throughout the Dominions, would be outraged by the profanation of the throne, also anathematized Mrs Simpson. On 27 November the Cabinet rejected the morganatic scheme. The Dominion leaders, invited somewhat tendentiously to give their views, more or less followed the British government's line. At the Bradford Diocesan Conference on 1 December Bishop Alfred Blunt, aware of the Defender of the Faith's entanglement with Mrs Simpson, voiced the wish that he would show more awareness of needing God's grace. The wall of silence was breached. The gentlemen-in-waiting of the press would wait no longer.

Their transition from quasi-courtiers to candid friends was hesitant and by no means complete. At first *The Times*, like most other papers, did not even mention Mrs Simpson by name; in a leading article full of unctuous circumlocution, it merely referred to 'a marriage incompatible with the THRONE'.[43] But soon the news emerged more starkly, shocking the nation and exposing the monarchy to unprecedented public controversy. *The Times* now declared that a woman with two husbands living was unfit to be queen, firmly articulating conservative and puritan opinion but by no means, as Lord Beaverbrook claimed, subjecting the king to a 'reign of terror'.[44] The Beaverbrook and Rothermere organs, along with other journals, took Edward's side. Accustomed to adulation, he was appalled by the mildest criticism and talked wildly of giving instructions to *The Times* and imposing restrictions on the BBC. His main concern, however, was to protect Wallis from public hostility: not only was she vilified as siren, harpy, Jezebel, but hate mail had been delivered to her door and stones flung through her windows. So on 3 December she left to stay with friends in Cannes, escorted by his trusted equerry Lord Brownlow and accompanied by jewellery worth a king's ransom. Edward's parting words reveal her as the lodestar of his life: 'I shall never give you up.'[45] His resolve did not waver. It frustrated last-ditch attempts to keep him on the throne and demonstrated that he was not jockeyed off it by an Establishment cabal led by Baldwin, Dawson and Lang – a view touted by Beaverbrook which still attracts conspiracy theorists today. The sole author of the abdication was Edward VIII himself.

The king was now under intense strain, smoking heavily, drinking whisky, losing the thread of discussions and sometimes cradling his head in his hands. That evening he asked the prime minister to be allowed to explain his position in a broadcast to the nation and then to await its verdict abroad. Baldwin, who was himself so distracted by the imbroglio that he refused to consider crucial matters of foreign policy, consulted the Cabinet, which promptly vetoed the request. Edward in turn forbade Beaverbrook to rally support in the country, where a so-called King's Party had briefly coalesced. It included demonstrators ranging from communist to fascist and doubtless represented a substantial body of popular opinion in favour of a royal love match. While Edward did nothing to encourage it, he was cheered by the chivalric support of Winston Churchill, whom his wife Clementine dubbed the last believer in the divine right of kings. He was also amused by Churchill's exhortation to barricade himself inside Windsor Castle. However the king did not accept his advice to endure and delay, wanting to go with dignity and without fuss. In fact, as Beaverbrook famously said to Churchill, 'Our cock won't fight.'[46]

Having formally confirmed his decision to Baldwin, Edward would not even fight at the behest of Wallis, who reached the Riviera on 6 December after a frenzied pursuit by reporters and photographers. Terrified of being blamed for damaging the monarchy, she implored him by airmail and badgered him over bad telephone lines not to abdicate. She also issued a public offer to withdraw from the situation herself. This and other initiatives made no difference. By 7 December feeling had hardened against a sovereign willing to abandon his subjects in order to gratify his passions. Churchill's plea for 'time and patience'[47] was shouted down in the Commons, a fierce rebuff which helped to discredit him at a time of mounting international peril. Edward in turn rejected his family's emotional entreaties to stay, telling his brother, the Duke of Kent, that he had known for two years that he could not 'stick' being king, that he 'could never tolerate the restrictions, the etiquette, the loneliness'.[48]

His mood veering between angst-ridden exhaustion and hectic gaiety, he now focused on securing a favourable abdication settlement. During fractious negotiations Edward demanded a pension of £25,000 a year, for which the new king would ultimately be responsible, in return for surrendering his life interest in Sandringham and Balmoral. He claimed that his fortune amounted to only £90,000, which was less than a tenth of the true figure. This lie, soon exposed and compounded by the subsequent dispute over the denial of royal status to Edward's future wife, would poison relations between the two brothers for the rest of their lives. Meanwhile the last procedures were completed. The instrument of abdication was signed on 10 December in the presence of Edward's three brothers. He accepted his new title, HRH the Duke of Windsor. Churchill arrived to improve his final address to the nation, murmuring tearfully on departure one of his favourite couplets, written by Andrew Marvell about the execution of Charles I:

> He nothing common did or mean,
> Upon that memorable scene.[49]

Edward's broadcast, heard with breathless attention throughout his realm on the evening of 11 December, also contained a poignant valediction: 'I have found it impossible to carry the heavy burden of responsibility and to discharge my duties as King as I would wish to do without the help and support of the woman I love.'[50]

# 5
# The Duke of Windsor at Bay

'In the darkness he left these shores.' Thus spoke Archbishop Lang in his own wireless oration, remarking on the coincidence that Edward quit the throne on the very day that King James II had fled the country in 1688. Lang further observed that Edward had surrendered his sacred trust because of a 'craving for private happiness' inconsistent with Christian principles of marriage and amid 'a social circle whose standards and ways of life are alien to all the best instincts and traditions of his people'.[1] Lang's sanctimonious homily was widely condemned, for the Duke of Windsor retained a prehensile hold on the imagination of many of his former subjects. Walter Monckton was not alone in saying, in a letter to Queen Mary, that 'there always will be a greatness and a glory about him'.[2] Mass Observation, a pioneering public opinion survey, found that at the time of George VI's coronation people 'really *liked*' the duke 'whatever his shortcomings',[3] and even during the war he remained a more attractive figure than the king. On the other hand, Lang was not just the voice of Victorian prudery, as intoned in church or, still more, in chapel. He spoke for many who felt that Edward had inflicted a grave wound in the heart of the British polity. Their outrage was well expressed by the Liberal social reformer Violet Markham: 'What will history say of a man who held an American harlot of more importance than the welfare of the nation or the Empire?'[4] Conservative courtiers were determined that the duke should do no more harm. None was more uncompromising than Tommy Lascelles, who maintained that Edward lacked moral and mental faculties to set against his 'exceptionally strong primitive passions'.[5] Moreover he had no aesthetic or spiritual capacities. Like the child in the fairy story, he was 'given everything in the world, but they forgot the soul'.[6]

Certainly the god in the constitutional machine had been shown to have feet of clay. The abdication crisis had administered, as the right-wing bishop Hensley Henson said, 'a serious shock to monarchical sentiment'.[7] For the first time in sixty years, wrote the left-wing academic Harold Laski, 'the validity of the monarchical principle itself is being widely discussed'.[8] The spectre of republicanism even raised its head in the House of Commons. Yet only five MPs were willing to vote to have an elected head of state. And Edward's blow against the hereditary principle never produced, as Churchill had feared, 'a profound lesion in the unity of this country'.[9] Nevertheless, George VI told his older brother that he had succeeded to a tottering throne and he doubted his ability to sustain it, let alone to restore the mystique of monarchy. His doubts were commonly shared: Lloyd George considered him 'a nitwit',[10] the French premier Édouard Daladier called him 'a moron'[11] and even Edward thought him 'a complete nincompoop'.[12] The new king's task was doubly difficult because at any time he could be outshone by the duke, who had always been the sun to his moon. Thus began a huge endeavour, backed by the 'forces most influential in molding mass opinion',[13] to create George VI in the image of his father: safe, punctilious, dignified, old-fashioned, a paragon of official probity and domestic virtue. Its corollary was a 'campaign of obliteration'[14] against the Duke of Windsor. The mass media, which could not attack him without impugning the monarchy itself, did their best to erase Edward's memory, to make him 'the world's prize forgotten man'.[15] Most newspapers treated him as 'a negative quantity without importance in British affairs'.[16] The 1937 *Annual Register* did not mention him at all. Newsreel companies wiped him from cinema screens. Gramophone records of the abdication broadcast were prevented from going on sale. The duke himself not only faced exile from his country but, as he would soon discover, ostracism by his family.

He crossed the Channel from Portsmouth aboard a destroyer, HMS *Fury*, cheerfully sending farewell cables at the navy's expense and expecting to return home with Wallis in a couple of years to act as a supernumerary prince. More immediately he had to avoid anything resembling collusion so that her divorce could be decreed absolute. So while Wallis remained in France he spent a fretful few months in Austria, mostly as the guest of Baroness Rothschild at Schloss Enzesfeld. To his chagrin none of his staff had been willing to accompany him abroad, though Fruity Metcalfe remained loyal and a Scotland Yard detective served as his bodyguard – and reported on his activities. The duke spent his time sightseeing, dog-walking, golfing, skiing, playing poker and skittles, shopping in Vienna, writing letters and bellowing down international telephone lines. Conversations with the king, punctuated by pauses, were especially fraught. The duke proffered gratuitous advice, haggled over money and pestered him to admit Wallis into the royal circle. But the two queens, Mary and Elizabeth, backed by courtiers, insisted that accepting her would dishonour the monarchy, and the king soon refused to take further calls from his brother. The duke was enraged and his growing antagonism towards his family was fostered by daily, sometimes hourly, communications with Wallis. It was a measure of her political sophistication that she had wondered if, after ceasing to be king, he could remain Emperor of India. All the same she convinced Edward that he was the victim of a deep-laid plot to eliminate and humiliate him. In particular she warned that King George 'would not give us the extra chic of creating me HRH'.[17] But what seemed a glittering fashion accessory to Wallis was to Edward not just an emblem of rank but a token of the love for which he had relinquished his patrimony. Its denial vexed his spirit and cast a permanent blight on his happiness.

The duke was reunited with Wallis on 4 May 1937, the day after her divorce proceedings were complete, at the Château de Candé in Touraine. This romantic retreat had been lent to them by Charles Bedaux, a rich Franco-American businessman, and they planned to be married there after George VI's coronation. That ceremony, on which unprecedented sums had been lavished, they heard on the wireless on 12 May, the duke expressing no regrets and knitting a blue sweater for Wallis. Churchill told him that the occasion had been a 'brilliant success'[18] and, dazzled by the radiant queen, he acknowledged to his wife that Wallis would not have done after all. And while remaining deeply respectful to the duke, Churchill privately disparaged his 'court of dagos on the Loire'.[19] Compared to the Abbey crowning, the château wedding, which took place in an improvised chapel on 3 June, was a sadly low-key affair. None of the duke's brothers attended and, fearing frowns from the Palace, even friends such as Brownlow and Mountbatten found reason to refuse their invitations. Queen Mary sent no present and the king's gift was a letter containing specious legal reasons for withholding the royal title from the duchess. Only with difficulty was an Anglican clergyman found to conduct the service and Fruity Metcalfe had to act as best man. The duke, his wife snubbed and himself shunned, could never forgive his family. But he exulted in having married the woman who, as Churchill said, was 'as necessary to his happiness as the air he breathed'.[20]

Accompanied by 186 trunks and eighty additional items of luggage, the Windsors went off to another loaned castle, Wasserleonburg in Carinthia, where they had an idyllic honeymoon. Then they based themselves in Paris, staying at the Hôtel Meurice. Here the duke had nothing to do except rehearse his grievances and yearn for an end to his exile. Admittedly Wallis filled his life to an extraordinary degree, but he did not contemplate an existence of indolent obscurity. In fact he was eager to resume his place in the limelight, co-starring with his consort. So it was that the duke made the worst blunder of his career. In October 1937 he accepted an invitation, arranged by Charles Bedaux, who had commercial reasons for ingratiating himself with the Nazis, to visit Hitler's Germany. Nominally this was a private tour to study workers' housing and labour conditions. But the Nazis, predictably keen to squeeze every ounce of propaganda from the duke's presence, turned it into an official progress.

The Windsors travelled in Hitler's personal train. Everywhere they were greeted by enthusiastic crowds. The duchess was accorded the royal title. The duke's inspection of Nazi industrial and architectural showpieces was given intensive coverage by Goebbels's publicity machine, which made much of his pro-German and anti-communist views. Not everything went according to plan. The Windsors' thuggish host, Robert Ley, head of the German Labour Front, got so drunk that he drove them at speed in his Mercedes through closed factory gates. And the duke saw maps indicating Germany's territorial ambitions. But Göring was monstrously genial and the Führer treated his guests with due courtesy, perhaps envisaging that he might use the ex-king as a pawn in his European strategy. When appearing in British newsreels the duke was cheered at home, but they omitted footage of his 'Heil Hitler' salutes and Fleet Street played down the whole visit. At court, though, everyone effervesced with indignation, asserting that the duke had behaved abominably, breaking his promise not to embarrass his brother and 'dropping bombshell after bombshell'. He was 'trying to stage a come-back, and his friends and advisers were semi-Nazis'.[21] King George was especially apprehensive about the duke's plan to extend his study tour to the United States. However American trade unions attacked his sponsor – Charles Bedaux again – as the champion of ruthless business efficiency techniques. And the American press criticized the duke for fraternizing with a brutal anti-Semitic regime and thus strengthening its hold over the masses. He therefore called off the US trip. 'Poor little man,' wrote a well-informed Scot, Lord Crawford. 'He has no sense of his own and no friends with any sense to advise him.'[22]

Actually the duke did have sensible friends, but he seldom listened to their advice. He had intended to ignore Churchill's warning, for example, that by crossing the Atlantic aboard the *Bremen*, instead of the *Normandie*, he risked offending 'millions of Jews'.[23] The duke was culpably naïve about the Nazis. He had no conception of their barbarism and twenty years after the Holocaust he could say, 'I never thought that Hitler was such a bad chap.'[24] Still, for a time the duke was inclined to heed Beaverbrook's counsel to step outside the public arena, having been mocked as well as scorned for his proposed 'slumming party': one American cartoon depicted him leaning on a trunk with labels saying St James's Palace, Honeymoon Castle, Château de Candé, Paris Hotels, with a billboard behind him announcing 'Duke of Windsor to Study Housing'.[25] Ironically he added to his domestic tally in 1938, leasing an elegant mansion at 24 boulevard Suchet in Paris and a palatial villa, Château de la Croë, near Antibes. In this constricted realm Wallis reigned supreme,

glorying in regal luxury – antique furniture, exotic bibe-
lots, theatrical décor, delicious food and a retinue of
well-drilled servants dressed in scarlet liveries with gold
collars, cuffs and buttons. Indeed, while Edward imposed
'rigid standards of etiquette'[26] such as he had earlier
spurned, she took on the patina of royalty, becoming
noticeably gracious, seeming to expect a curtsey and angli-
cizing her accent. Everywhere the duke, whose own accent
was a curious mélange of patrician, Cockney and American, followed her with adoring eyes. He had little else to
occupy his time apart from recreation, entertainment and
the occasional puerile practical joke. Having installed a
toilet roll dispenser which played 'God Save the King'
when the paper was unwound, he would wait outside the
lavatory door and shout at unsuspecting guests, 'Stand to
Attention!'[27]

Despite such attempts at good cheer, Walter Monckton
found the atmosphere around the duke after a year of ban-
ishment 'even more combative and aggrieved than usual'.[28]
His financial wrangle with the king, involving legal men-
aces, corrosive suspicions and charges of bad faith on both
sides, became still more acrimonious when the government
attempted to make payment of a reduced pension dependent on the Duke of Windsor's undertaking not to return
home without official permission. He protested vocifer-
ously against this insulting condition, which was softened
in a settlement finalized in February 1938. The following
month, claiming to have been denied proper acknowledge-
ment for contributing to an effigy of George V, he said that
his last vestiges of family feeling had been destroyed. But it

was clear that the royal embargo on the Windsors would continue. Courtiers discouraged the British ambassador in Paris from inviting the duke to diplomatic functions. Queen Mary prevented the Duke of Kent from meeting him. Queen Elizabeth, nicknamed 'Cookie' by Wallis on account of her supposed resemblance to a 'fat Scotch cook',[29] referred to the duchess as 'that woman'.[30] When the king and queen paid a state visit to France in July 1938, the duke was excluded from the proceedings. In the autumn he did see his dim sibling Henry, but all his efforts to return home were blocked. For the time being, at any rate, Edward was to remain the ex-king over the water.

His family's obduracy, as critics noted, by no means advertised Buckingham Palace as a fount of Christian charity. Queen Elizabeth, who in her resentment over the strain involuntary kingship had imposed on her husband doubtless exaggerated Wallis's aptitude for intrigue and vendetta, was especially implacable. The duke was not alone in detecting granite beneath her sugar coating – Cecil Beaton memorably described her as 'a marshmallow made on a welding machine'.[31] Yet the king and queen had understandable reasons for keeping the duke at a distance. Like Queen Caroline of Brunswick before him and Diana Princess of Wales later, he was a royal loose cannon. He had a significant capacity to inflict damage upon the throne, particularly as its occupant was so frail and insecure. In one shattering gaffe at the end of 1937, for example, the duke reportedly told a journalist that he was prepared, if the Labour Party wished it, to become president of a future English republic – thus appearing as a kind of

Citizen Pretender. Similarly the duke's broadcast to the world from Verdun, the most terrible killing field of the First World War, seemed well calculated to upset King George. The sentiments were unexceptionable: speaking as a soldier who had served on the Western Front, the duke earnestly prayed that such 'cruel and destructive madness shall never again overtake mankind'.[32] But the timing was deplorable: he took to the airwaves on 8 May 1939, just as the king and queen were sailing to North America on a mission of goodwill. The duke was widely blamed for attempting to overshadow his successor and the BBC refused to relay the broadcast. Ironically, though, both royal brothers wanted peace at almost any price and both ardently supported Neville Chamberlain's policy of appeasing Hitler. But whereas the Foreign Office stopped the king from sending the Führer a plea for peace as 'one ex-Serviceman to another',[33] the duke despatched just such a personal appeal on 27 August. Needless to say, it was futile: the Nazi-Soviet Pact had been signed and Germany was poised to invade Poland. Yet the duke never ceased to maintain that 'if I'd been king, there'd have been no war'.[34]

The outbreak of hostilities in September gave him an opportunity not only to serve his country but also to open a new campaign on behalf of the duchess. When the king offered to send an aircraft to bring them back from the Riviera, the duke initially refused to come unless they were received at a royal residence. Even Fruity Metcalfe was appalled by such a stipulation at such a time, accusing them of behaving like spoilt brats: 'women & children are being bombed & killed while *you* talk of your PRIDE'.[35]

Apparently chastened, they did return – aboard Mountbatten's destroyer, HMS *Kelly*, sent by Winston Churchill, who was once more First Lord of the Admiralty. The two queens cold-shouldered the duke. But he did have a short meeting with the king, who found him characteristically ebullient, though 'he seemed to be thinking only of himself & had quite forgotten what he had done to his country in 1936'.[36] Still, there were no recriminations as they kept off contentious topics. The duke accepted an appointment as a Major-General, though he was reluctant to give up permanently his honorary rank of Field Marshal. He wanted a job at home but, with Chamberlain's connivance, he was quickly hustled across the Channel as a member of the British Military Mission liaising with the French high command. The duke's role was both contrived and restricted since, in Lord Crawford's words, 'He is too irresponsible as a chatterbox to be entrusted with confidential information, which will be passed on to Wally at the dinner table.'[37]

In carrying out his war work, however, the duke could not win. When succeeding, he seemed to upstage his brother; when failing, he let down the monarchy. In the event his achievements were mixed. He made a good impression on the French and was given unique access to their defences. He then wrote four perceptive (but ignored) reports exposing their weakness, noting the poor state of morale and discipline in General Gamelin's army, and casting doubt on the impregnability of the Maginot Line. The duke was also warmly received when he visited the headquarters of the British Expeditionary Force near

Arras on 18 October. Exalted by the acclaim, however, he made the mistake of taking salutes intended for the commander-in-chief, Lord Gort. As a result he was told that his tours of inspection must be confined to the French sector. This provoked an explosion of wrath. According to the duchess, the Windsors were fighting two wars and in the one against Buckingham Palace 'no quarter was given'.[38] Proposing to accuse the king of pusillanimity and unbrotherly hatred, the duke demanded a personal interview. He was fobbed off and Churchill urged him to treat small matters of precedence and ceremony as beneath his dignity, thus clothing himself in 'impenetrable armour'.[39] But such matters loomed large in the duke's mind. And he had some justification for feeling persecuted, rightly inferring that the king turned Fort Belvedere over to the government in February 1940 as a preliminary to reneging on his verbal agreement to reserve it for his brother. The duke spent the rest of the Phoney War nursing his bile, performing his limited duties more or less adequately, hankering for a negotiated peace and when possible seeing Wallis in Paris. As she wrote to a friend, 'We are both thoroughly disgusted and fed up in every way but are caught like rats in a trap until the war ends.'[40]

On 10 May Hitler turned on the Low Countries and France, and so swiftly did his panzers advance that, less than a week later, the duke drove Wallis to Biarritz. He returned to Paris briefly but, unwilling to leave her alone, soon went south again, filling his cars with valuables and abandoning his senior staff without a word. Convinced that Edward had piled desertion on abdication, Fruity

Metcalfe left his service in disgust. In fact the duke had got permission to link with the *Armée des Alpes* facing Mussolini's forces. But as France collapsed the Windsors fled to neutral Spain, arriving in Madrid on 23 June, the duke's forty-sixth birthday. Here the British ambassador was his old friend Sam Hoare, who found him an awkward guest.

The duke kept anti-British company. Although usually wary, he let slip enough defeatist sentiments to reach German ears. And when Churchill summoned him back to England, the duke tried to impose conditions. He demanded an end to the family feud, a meeting with the king at which the duchess would be present, a job with royal backing and compensation from the Civil List if he lost his tax-free status. Hoare told him that 'when the world is crashing this is no time for bargaining'.[41] But the duke's egocentricity verged on solipsism. He complied only when Churchill reminded him that he was a serving officer whose refusal to obey orders would have serious consequences – a threat its recipient thought gangsterish. Thus on 2 July the Windsors drove to Portugal, but before they could fly home Churchill offered the duke the governorship of the Bahamas. He accepted reluctantly. The duchess quipped that the appointment was a disappointment and the duke dubbed the Caribbean archipelago 'St Helena 1940!'.

They spent the month before their departure in a seaside villa near Lisbon, entirely preoccupied with their own affairs. The duchess told her aunt that 'one's time is spent trying to communicate with France to make some arrangements for one's houses'. Through Spanish intermediaries the duke asked the Axis powers to protect his property. He also requested permission from the Germans to retrieve his belongings from France, shocking even Franco's brother who remarked: 'A prince does not ask favours of his country's enemies.'[42] Moreover the duke continued to harass the embattled Churchill. He wished to visit New York before going on to Nassau and he wanted his batman, Alistair Fletcher, to be released from military duties in order to serve as his valet – he later admitted to being helpless without one. Fearing that the duke might encourage American isolationism, the prime minister refused to permit the US detour. But after an exasperating wrangle he gave way over the batman – Lascelles and Monckton said that there was 'serious danger of an explosion'[43] over this issue and that the duke 'had to be treated as a petulant baby'.[44]

Meanwhile the Germans were weaving a web of conspiracy around the Windsors so intricate that even now it is hard to distinguish fact from fantasy. Preparing his cross-Channel invasion, Hitler became convinced that he could somehow use the duke to divide and rule Britain. So Spanish emissaries were despatched to inveigle him back to Spain, where he could be kidnapped by German commandos. And Hitler's secret agents took measures to scare him into returning, not least by spreading the rumour that Churchill planned to have him assassinated. Their plot failed, though the Germans did manage to detain the duchess's maid as she struggled through occupied France with trunks full of her employers' possessions. By 1 August the American steamship *Excalibur* had gone with the Windsors.

It is impossible to know whether the duke could have been persuaded, bribed or coerced into becoming, as

Hitler probably hoped, a Quisling king of England. Edward clearly admired the Third Reich and expected it to win, so he might have been willing to act as a puppet in order to stop the slaughter and secure a settlement with Germany. He could thus have regarded himself as a patriot king, much as Victor Emmanuel did in fascist Italy, or a national saviour, much as Marshal Pétain did in France. However it is almost inconceivable that the duke would have consciously betrayed his country. He loved it, revered it, pined for it. When a draft message to Dominion leaders stated that the duke's 'inclinations are well-known to be pro-Nazi' Churchill altered it to say that his loyalties were 'unimpeachable'.[45] Yet even Churchill had his doubts and he did refer, in conversation with King George, to his brother's 'pro-Nazi leanings'.[46] Furthermore the prime minister sent the duke off with a solemn warning that reports of his incautious talk had reached London and that as an officer of the crown he should be careful not to express opinions different from those of His Majesty's Government, particularly at a time of such 'immense stress and dire peril'.[47] The duke replied that he would bear Churchill's counsel in mind, notably in the hazardous field of American politics. But he proposed to take occasional periods of leave in the United States since 'you perfectly appreciate how impossible it would be for me to be anchored indefinitely within the limits of the Bahamas'.[48] It was an ominous proviso. During Britain's finest hour the duke had shown little magnanimity and less wisdom; and though his record now improved, he would find as a colonial governor further scope for folly.

# 6

# Governor of the Bahamas

No sooner had the duke come into his miniature kingdom than he wanted to leave it, thus striking the first note in a dominant theme of his five-year governorship. To escape the stifling heat and humidity of New Providence Island in August, he asked permission from the Colonial Secretary Lord Lloyd to take the duchess to his Canadian ranch for a few weeks. Lloyd refused on the ground that the duke had only just taken up his post. With characteristic pertinacity the duke then requested £5,000 for refurbishing the run-down Government House in Nassau, 'to ensure some dignity during my term of office'.[1] Lloyd would not oblige, silkily replying that he wanted 'to protect your Royal Highness from any accusation, however ill-founded, of extravagant expenditure', not least since critics could say (as the Battle of Britain raged) that the money 'might have been used to buy a fighter'.[2] More galling still, the duke learned of the Colonial Office's instruction that the duchess was not to be addressed as a Royal Highness or to receive curtseys in the Bahamas. Contemplating resignation, he blamed this humiliation on the vindictive jealousy of Queen Elizabeth. It added to his near-paranoid conviction that since becoming king he had been the victim of a

Machiavellian campaign conducted by 'Official England', which had first forced him off the throne and now marooned him on a desert island. The Windsors hated the place. The duchess, who found the locals petty-minded and the visitors 'common and uninteresting', described it variously as a 'dump' and a 'moron paradise'.[3] The duke disparaged the calibre and intellect of his associates and told Churchill that unless given access to the mainland he would seem 'vitually [*sic*] a prisoner here'.[4]

For all his whinges, though, the duke presented a brave face to the 70,000 inhabitants of the barren islands scattered between Florida and Cuba that constituted his domain. Most Bahamians were black and half lived in Nassau, where they cheered the arrival of the Windsors. The sweating duke declared that he was delighted by the warmth of their welcome. The duchess, poised and elegant, exuded charm – to say nothing of fragrant Parisian scent. The couple quickly made their presence felt. With a grant from the local legislature plus a contribution of their own, they renovated and redecorated Government House, where they dispensed gracious hospitality to suitable guests. Actually the Windsors thought it degrading to have to greet visitors, but tourism was the prime source of Bahamian revenue and they felt bound to act as the star attraction. Everywhere, in fact, they stooped to conquer. The duke rode around Nassau on a bicycle and made self-deprecating jokes – displaying some new swimming trunks he remarked, 'It's I, you see, who wear the shorts in this family.'[5] The duchess established and supervised Red Cross clinics. Together they promoted and patronized a host of local events and activities, sports, bazaars, exhibitions, concerts and so on, concentrating on charitable enterprises. Both were shocked by the obtrusive poverty and squalor in what was one of the most neglected of Britain's imperial slums. As a dyed-in-the-wool paternalist, the duke was keen to make improvements in housing, education and welfare. Above all he aimed to provide more employment, encouraging investment and agriculture in the outer islands, and setting up a training centre called Windsor Farm. Such modest initiatives aroused opposition from the white oligarchy which controlled the legislature, a clique of reactionary merchants known as the Bay Street Boys. But the duke sparked extravagant hopes among the blacks, one of whom, according to the travel writer Rosita Forbes, hailed his advent in stereotypical fashion: 'De Lawd comes! Hallelujah, 'tis de Lawd!'

This salutation was calculated to appeal to the Windsors, whose racial prejudices were pronounced. 'We Southerners,' the duchess laughingly told Rosita Forbes, 'always flatter ourselves we know best how to deal with coloured people.'[6] Among her techniques, which aroused local ire, was the disparagement of Bahamian girls' clothes and the banning of blacks from canteens in her infant welfare centres. The duke also endorsed racial segregation, which had recently become more severe in order to meet the requirements of American tourists. A colour bar prevailed at Government House and on the Executive Council. The duke objected to an 'all-coloured police force',[7] wanting British constables to patrol white areas. He supported racial discrimination in employment and according to

Étienne Dupuch, the outspoken editor of the *Nassau Trib-une*, he would rather lose the war than sanction black advancement. The duke advised Dupuch that it was not done to criticize royalty, denounced him as a half-caste agitator and tried to get him sacked from his job as a cor-respondent for the Associated Press. As governor, he deplored the Colonial Office's more liberal approach towards race relations and all talk of self-government. That must come in the end, but the premature airing of socialistic ideas about freedom and equality was danger-ous. Those with experience of a large coloured population, he told Churchill, coining a cliché that reflected the prime minister's own prejudices, 'realize that negroes in the mass are still children both mentally and morally'.[8]

Whereas the duke wished to raise them up, however, the Bay Street Boys aimed to keep them in a permanent state of tutelage. For them the black inhabitants were essentially a source of cheap labour and any improvement in their helot condition posed a threat to white supremacy. And since the Bay Street Boys controlled the House of Assem-bly, and thus held the purse strings, they were able to frustrate the duke's proposals to foster public works and create jobs. This was one reason for his cultivation of prominent businessmen willing to pump money into the Bahamian economy, such as the Canadian gold-mining magnate Sir Harry Oakes and the Swedish Electrolux mil-lionaire Axel Wenner-Gren. The latter was an objectionable associate since he had recently attempted to broker a peace through Göring and the American authorities considered him 'a dangerous pro-Nazi'.[9] There was little hard evidence of this but the duke persistently ignored warnings to shun the Swede. Indeed, he created a deplorable impression in December 1940 by sailing to Miami aboard Wenner-Gren's magnificent yacht. The Windsors wooed the American crowds with their usual skill and refused to attend banquets because Britain was at war. But they remained incorrigibly indiscreet. The duchess had let it be known that the Bahamas failed to provide scope for her husband's great gifts, while he blurted out that it was 'too late for America to save Democracy in Europe'.[10] He thus gave comfort to American non-interventionists at a time when, as Churchill would remind him, 'Our dearest wish and greatest need in this country is to have the United States enter the war.'[11]

The duke's most egregious error was to give an interview in March 1941 to Fulton Oursler, editor of the American magazine *Liberty*, which would be taken, Churchill wrote, as 'defeatist and pro-Nazi'.[12] The duke subscribed to the view that you could not kill or coerce the eighty million Germans, who 'want Hitler'. He would inevitably 'moderate his policies'.[13] So the time had come, the duke agreed, for someone to say: 'You boys stop fighting and make up.'[14] In response to Churchill's reprimand, the duke claimed that words had been put into his mouth and he threatened to resign. But Oursler informed Lord Halifax, British ambassador in Washington, that the 'manuscript was submitted to the Duke before publication and received his approval'.[15] And the prime minister was in no mood to listen to excuses, let alone to pussyfoot. Ignoring the suggestion of Lord Moyne, the new Colonial

Secretary, that their mutual friend might feel affronted by the severity of his language, Churchill told the duke that his remarks could 'only bear the meaning of contemplating a negotiated peace with Hitler'.[16] This was not the government's policy, any more such interviews would harm British interests and he could leave the Bahamas only when his public utterances were more conformist. The duke was not so much affronted as enraged. In a long, bitter and cogent telegram he dwelt on his past experience of handling reporters and said that he must be allowed to visit America. Counter-attacking, he complained of a recent article in *Life* magazine in which Queen Elizabeth had referred to the duchess as 'that Woman', an insult that compounded 'the chronic anomaly of my wife not having the same official status as myself'. If only his family were willing to accept her, he would be 'proud to share' the sacrifices and sufferings of his countrymen at home. The tone of Churchill's messages, the duke concluded, made it hard for him 'to believe that you are still the friend you used to be'.[17]

Concerned that American newspapers might portray the Windsors as martyrs, the prime minister quickly relented. The duke, conceding that Churchill was all-powerful, got leave to make an extended autumn trip to Canada and the United States, where he undertook not to talk politics since it was 'far too dangerous'.[18] Elaborate efforts were made to hold him to this assurance. His movements were regulated. He was given an experienced press officer, René MacColl, to keep journalists at bay. Churchill personally drafted a brilliant statement for him to deliver, which concluded that the English-speaking nations would eventually guide mankind out of 'the dark valleys of death and destruction'.[19] Apart from this the duke stuck mainly to platitudes and President Roosevelt, who had a weakness for royalty, found that he was now more robust on the subject of war and victory. The Windsors were fêted like film stars and their tour was a spectacular success.

But they did not entirely avoid trouble. The duke altered his itinerary without Halifax's approval and ostentatiously dismissed MacColl so that he could speak to reporters alone. Swathed in finery, the duchess said that she was not all that interested in clothes and shopping. With their seventy-three pieces of luggage and twenty-three retainers the couple were criticized for 'dreamboat extravagance', especially when they took a suite at the Waldorf Towers in New York's 'Millionaire Stratosphere'. The *World-Telegram* alleged that the embarrassed British government was 'on the verge of repudiating them publicly'.[20] Actually the duke, who would ask the FBI to find out if the author of a hostile article in the *American Mercury* was Jewish, felt like repudiating his own kin. A few weeks before Japan bombed Pearl Harbor, he told Halifax that 'he never wanted to see them again'. He was, however, 'completely happy with the most wonderful wife in the world'.[21]

America's entry into the war snuffed out the Windsors' defeatism and offered the Bahamas a ray of hope in a time of Depression. Compensating for the collapse of the tourist industry, the construction of two American air bases generated thousands of new jobs. However the Bahamian government negotiated an agreement whereby local

1. Queen Victoria with the future Kings George V, Edward VII and Edward VIII, 1899. She found her great-grandson 'a most attractive little boy, and so forward and clever'.

2. The Prince of Wales's investiture at Caernarfon, 1911. Although embarrassed by his 'fantastic costume', he performed well in the invented ceremony.

3. The bonnie prince with the Black Watch, 1918. He did wonders for military morale but was embittered by being kept out of the front line.

4. Edward in Launceston, Australia, 1920. His imperial tours, unprecedented in scope, were spectacularly successful but they shredded his nerves.

5. Setting the style as Captain of the Royal & Ancient Golf Club, St Andrews, 1922.

6. Freda Dudley Ward, 1918. Edward called her 'my precious lovely little Madonna' and said that even her photograph inspired him to 'naughtiness'.

7. The prince in 1932 with Thelma Furness, who succeeded Freda as his mistress.

8. King Edward with Mrs Simpson, Dalmatian coast, 1936.
Photographs of their summer cruise, unpublished in Britain,
alerted the world to the royal affair.

9. The king at Boverton, Glamorgan, 18 November 1936. Although
urging and offering assistance for distressed areas, he had already
decided to abdicate.

10. A 1936 postcard commemorating the monarchy's *annus horribilis*. Afterwards the British authorities tried to expunge Edward from the public mind.

11. Foreign journals celebrated the glamour and romance of the Windsors' wedding, but it was boycotted by Edward's family and virtually all his friends.

12. The Duke of Windsor's self-promoting visit to Hitler's Germany in 1937 confirmed his pro-Nazi sympathies.

13 and 14. The Windsors escaped to Madrid in June 1940. Wallis sports a flamingo brooch of rubies, sapphires, emeralds and diamonds, specially made by Cartier.

15. The duke had a mixed record as wartime Governor of the Bahamas and chafed incessantly against his exile.

16. The prime minister, ever loyal, welcomes the duke to 10 Downing Street, 1953. But even Churchill could not settle the royal family feud.

17. The pug-besotted Windsors in the grounds of their Paris mansion adjoining the Bois de Boulogne, 1964. It was run like a miniature Versailles.

18. After the war the duke had little to occupy his time. Apparently in pensive mood, he sits outside his country house, the Moulin de la Tuilerie, 1955.

labourers were paid just four shillings a day, which was hardly a living wage and amounted to only half the sum earned by workers brought in from the mainland. In June 1942 a mass protest sparked off two days of rioting in Nassau. Several people were killed and much of the Bay Street commercial district was looted and burnt. The duke was in Washington at the time and initially tried to suppress news of the trouble, which he blamed on Jews and communists. However he at once flew back to the Bahamas, where he made a conciliatory broadcast and increased wages to five shillings a day. He also enforced a curfew, banned public meetings, censored the press and accepted a detachment of American Marines offered by Roosevelt, thus equipping himself with the firepower, as he told Churchill, to deal with any further 'negro disturbances'.[22] None occurred, but there was a prolonged wrangle about the underlying cause of the riot and the reforms needed to maintain order. The duke rightly concluded that the pay dispute was merely an excuse for the violence, which was motivated by 'strong racial feeling on both sides'.[23] But although he wanted fairer labour laws and a more equitable tax regime, he resisted substantial measures, such as the introduction of a secret ballot, calculated to end white oppression. In any case the Bay Street caucus ensured that his reforms were modest. However the war demanded labour and the duke got an accord from Washington that some 5,000 Bahamians should be recruited to work in the United States. The scheme employed a sixth of all males on the islands and helped to transform their economy. It has been deemed a 'momentous achievement'.[24]

Unfortunately for the duke it was eclipsed by the cause célèbre of his governorship, the murder of Sir Harry Oakes. This took place on 8 July 1943 when the wealthiest baronet in the empire was bludgeoned to death in his bed and his corpse covered with feathers and set alight. The duke assumed personal charge of the situation and proceeded to make a series of abysmal blunders. He tried unsuccessfully to muzzle the press. Doubting the competence of the local police, he brought in two detectives from Miami who bungled the investigation and fabricated fingerprint evidence. The duke, who had jumped to the conclusion that Oakes's playboy son-in-law, Alfred de Marigny, was guilty of the murder, evidently encouraged his arrest. But in court the prosecution case was so flawed that the jury acquitted Marigny, though it recommended that he should be deported. The duke, who had retreated to America during the trial, was deeply humiliated by the verdict and made every effort to expel Marigny. But he could find no legal grounds for doing so though he argued, with unconscious irony, that Marigny's matrimonial history, which consisted of two divorces and three marriages, showed 'him to be an unscrupulous adventurer'.[25] Among other suspects were business associates, Mafia hitmen and voodoo cultists, but no one has ever been convicted of Oakes's killing, which remains a mystery. It not only spawned sensational headlines at the time but has given rise to conspiracy theories ever since. A persistent one is that the duke was involved with Oakes in illegal foreign exchange trading and so prevented a proper homicide inquiry. Latterly Marigny himself claimed that the duke had participated in 'a plot to send an innocent man to his death'.[26] Although Edward was quite capable of financial dishonesty, there is no proof of any such charges. Indeed, the likelihood is that, once again, he played the part of a fool rather than a knave.

It is indisputable, though, that his reputation was badly damaged by the Oakes fiasco. Nothing confirmed the governor's lack of judgement more dramatically or disqualified him more decisively from obtaining the kind of move he craved. As the tide of war turned in favour of the Allies, the Windsors became increasingly desperate about their own plight, complaining that they had been buried alive and left to rot in 'this awful hot depressing hole'.[27] They often escaped to the mainland, which offered some alleviation of their miseries, particularly when, during an appendectomy, the duchess was found to have cancerous tumours in her stomach; they were successfully removed and she made a good recovery. The duke also met Churchill in America, missing no chance to importune him for a better job. In 1943, after considering other far-flung options, the prime minister offered him the governorship of Bermuda; but the duke thought the island too far from the United States and he rejected what was anyway hardly a promotion.

Ideally he wanted a roving commission in America, cooperating with the British ambassador but acting independently and enjoying tax-free status. The turmoil he might have caused as a rogue diplomat was all too apparent and the proposal, though long pursued, was eventually scotched. However Churchill did not abandon the Windsors and at the duke's insistence he made several efforts to heal the family rift. Although the duchess had written a placatory letter to Queen Mary, whose sons were united in their grief over the accidental death of the Duke of Kent, reconciliation still seemed unattainable. Churchill tried in vain to mollify the ex-king, imploring him not to attach undue importance to his wife's title 'after the immense renunciations you have made'.[28]

In September 1944 the two men met in Washington, where the duke got permission to resign his post. He hoped to return home and, with the prime minister's assistance, to make a fresh start. After all, he observed sardonically, British propagandists kept repeating that the king had established himself securely in the hearts of his people, so his predecessor could hardly steal the limelight whatever employment he obtained. And surely, in the effervescence of victory, his family could be persuaded 'to swallow "the Windsor pill" just once'.[29] In May 1945 the duke left the Bahamas for good, with a record which, though tarnished, was better than that of many colonial governors. He spent the rest of the summer in the United States, worrying about money (having lost 100,000 dollars drilling for non-existent oil on his Canadian ranch), bemoaning the advance of communism (notably in Britain, where the Labour Party triumphed at the polls), and planning a future that would not be entirely devoted to leisure.

In September the Windsors sailed to France, where they found their houses intact, and the duke then paid a visit to England, where he had a surprisingly amicable reunion with the king and Queen Mary. But they stuck to the line that, as Lascelles had put it, there was no official place in the British cosmos for an ex-king, whose presence would anyway be 'a constant agony (I use the word advisedly) to the present King'.[30] And as George VI recorded, their mother once again told the duke that she would never receive the duchess, 'as nothing has happened to alter the circumstances which had led to his abdication'. She spoke, added the king, in such a way that 'he could see this was final'.[31] The duke still hoped for some kind of official position representing Britain in the United States, particularly as the king was so anxious to put the Atlantic between them. But one by one the possibilities, which had included governorships in Madras and Ceylon, were extinguished. And by mid 1946 it was clear that the Duke of Windsor's public life had come to an end.

# 7
# Last Years

Having lost a crown, however, the duke did not easily give up hope of finding a role. Indeed, for seven years after the war he refused to settle down in France because he still felt there was a chance that he could return home or obtain some suitable post representing his country abroad. The duke disliked France and the French, whose language he spoke hesitantly and with such 'an utterly *appalling* accent'[1] that it was liable to be mistaken for English. But he was swayed by the immunity from taxation which the Republic had puzzlingly bestowed on the ex-king, a boon not available in America, which otherwise attracted the Windsors. So in 1946, their mansion in the boulevard Suchet having been sold, they re-established themselves at the Château de la Croë, where their needs were met by a staff of thirty. The duchess, thin to the point of emaciation but wearing no underclothes to look thinner still, struggled against post-war conditions to restore their mimic court to its pre-war standards – so much so that one guest wished somebody 'could tell her not to be such a perfect housekeeper'.[2] But the duke, lacking an occupation, was bored and restless. He might spend a morning having the dogs coiffed or watching the duchess buying a hat.

Afternoons were devoted to golf and evenings to entertainment. Then he would bewail the prospect of a Red future and gnaw over the past, declaring that he had been 'diddled out of the Crown ... by sinister influences'.[3] The Windsors also travelled a great deal, moving from place to place in the hope of getting somewhere. In the autumn of 1946 they paid a private visit to England, staying with the Earl of Dudley at Ednam Lodge in Berkshire, where a cat burglar stole most of the duchess's jewellery. She became hysterical, demanding that all the servants be 'put through a kind of third degree'.[4] The duke was still more disillusioned with his native land, but he used the insurance money to purchase a further cornucopia of gems.

In 1947 he found another way to make money and, equally important, to fill the vacant hours. He accepted a commission from *Life* magazine to write four long articles about his youth. The duke was provided with an accomplished journalist, Charles Murphy, to organize his free-flowing reminiscences and present them in literate form. Although this enterprise provoked anxiety and even outrage in Buckingham Palace, where the rule of *omertà* prevailed, the articles proved to be both lively and innocuous. Their favourable reception encouraged the duke to embark on a full-scale memoir. Soon he complained of being lashed to his desk, while the duchess asserted that they were complete slaves to the book. But Murphy, once again the ghostwriter, found it hard to get any consistent work out of the duke and the duchess regularly interrupted him with social and domestic demands. Moreover the couple, having been tormented by indecision about where to live, gave up La Croë in 1949 and rented another mansion, 85 rue de la Faisanderie, in Paris. This major upheaval tested even the duchess's powers of household management and it further delayed the writing.

To enable the duke to concentrate, she went to America in November 1950. But he moped in her absence, looking pathetic and saying that 'nothing is nice for him without the Duchess'.[5] His spirits fell further when the news broke that she was cavorting around New York with their infamous new friend Jimmy Donahue, a homosexual playboy and heir to the Woolworth fortune. So in December he suddenly resolved to join her. The querulous Murphy went too, apparently fearful during the voyage that the duke was in a suicidal mood. But his reunion with the duchess seemed joyous enough and by March 1951 *A King's Story* was finished. The Palace predictably disapproved of its publication and Churchill's crony Brendan Bracken thought the memoir 'deplorable stuff'.[6] But as apologias go the duke's was elegant, dignified, sometimes wryly humorous and (apart from a pronounced animus against Baldwin) benign. It got complimentary reviews, sold exceptionally well, topped up the duke's coffers and in 1965 became the basis for Jack Le Vien's documentary film, which was nominated for an Oscar.

Meanwhile the royal family continued to boycott the Windsors. Churchill contended that there were 'serious disadvantages in utterly casting off the Duke of Windsor from all official contact with Great Britain, and leaving him in a disturbed and distressed state of mind'.[7] But, now in opposition, he cut no ice in the Palace. Thus the duke and duchess were not invited to Princess Elizabeth's wedding. Queen Mary refused her eldest son's renewed plea to meet his wife. King George encouraged an amenable Clement Attlee to reject the duke's appeal, in 1949, against the legal ruling that denied the duchess her husband's rank. At a meeting later that year the duke apparently accused the king of hating him and making his life impossible. Writing afterwards, King George told his brother that he had renounced the throne in deference to the general view that his intended wife was not suitable to be queen and if she 'now became a member of our family, there is no reason why she should not have become your Queen in 1937. It wouldn't make sense of the past.'[8] The Windsors blamed a court clique for their exclusion, reckoning that by himself the king was too weak and stupid to justify his intransigence in such terms. This perhaps explains the vehemence of the duke's remarks about the Festival of Britain in 1951. He told his secretary Anne Seagrim that his brother was furious about this extravaganza yet he had to open it: 'That's one of the worst things about being King . . . you have to do things that you know are wrong – wrong – wrong – all wrong. That's Terrrrible.'[9]

In February 1951 the duchess was again successfully treated for cancer; a year later the king died of the same disease. The duke, who was in New York, sailed to England for the obsequies. He stayed with his grieving mother, who felt that now was the time to heal the family rift. She wrote to the widowed Queen Elizabeth, beseeching 'you & the girls to see him & to bury the hatchet after 15 years'.[10] The duke duly went to tea in Buckingham Palace and the duchess urged him to take advantage of his reception: 'Now that the door has been opened a crack try and get your foot in.'[11] He was positioned beside the other royal dukes in the funeral procession – clad in naval uniform, he was variously described as looking 'jaunty' and 'haunted by guilt'.[12] But although he had further meetings with the new sovereign, nothing had really changed and Queen Mary was quite wrong in her assumption that the feud had ended. The duchess remained a pariah and the duke now faced losing his brother's allowance. To his wife he expostulated, 'It's hell even to be even this much dependent on these ice-veined bitches.'

His rancour overflowed when he returned in March 1953 to see his mother during her final illness. Queen Mary was an unconscionable time a-dying and he wrote to Wallis that ice instead of blood 'must be a fine preservative'. The duke found the waiting hellish, chafed about his wife's absence and his mother's 'vile' behaviour towards her, and filled the time with golf, canasta, shopping and a point-to-point. Eventually, as he put it, the nightmare was over and after the funeral he laid claim to a number of Queen Mary's most valuable and interesting personal possessions. Lamenting that the 'vultures' in his family would have first pick when the spoils were actually divided, he declared: 'What a smug stinking lot my relations are.'[13] The Windsors were not invited to Queen Elizabeth II's coronation. But before he returned to New York, the duke completed an article on the subject. The duchess considered it a wonderfully generous build-up to the young queen and told Anne Seagrim that 'she thought he was a saint'.[14]

The duke wrote several other articles in similar vein, which he turned into a short book entitled *The Crown and the People 1902–1953*. Among other things it dwelt on the danger that the monarchy would be socially isolated by the impoverishment of the hereditary aristocracy, thanks to 'confiscatory taxation'.[15] A mark of the peers' reduced circumstances, he noted, was a court regulation permitting them to wear robes trimmed not with ermine but with rabbit. At this time the Windsors were more than usually exercised about money (prompting the duchess to embark on her own lucrative memoir, *The Heart Has Its Reasons*) because they had decided to put down permanent roots in France. In 1952 they acquired an old mill in the Chevreuse Valley, the Moulin de la Tuilerie, which became their country retreat, mainly used at weekends. Soon afterwards they accepted an offer from the city of Paris to lease on easy terms 4 route du Champ d'Entraînement, a mansion set in ample grounds on the edge of the Bois de Boulogne. For the next four years they spared no effort or expense to make these residences fit for an ex-king.

The Moulin was transformed into what one visitor, James Pope-Hennessy, called the duchess's Petit Trianon. As he recorded, 'Every conceivable luxury and creature comfort is brought, called on, conscripted, to produce a perfection of sybaritic living.'[16] The pièce de résistance was a huge converted barn crammed with memorabilia of the duke's life: silver statues of Queen Victoria, pig-sticking and steeplechasing trophies, drums of the Grenadier and Welsh Guards which served as occasional tables, a sample of every button used by the British army during the First

World War, an illuminated map showing his journeys as Prince of Wales, commemorative medals, regimental colours, framed addresses, Gurkha kukris, a thermometer from the apex of the Empire State Building, three silver-mounted golf balls which he had 'holed in one' and the Chippendale table, covered with royal photographs, on which he had signed the instrument of abdication. If the interiors were flamboyant, the thirty acres surrounding the mill resembled an Impressionist painting. As at Fort Belvedere, the duke devoted much of his time to vigorous horticulture, planting herbaceous borders, building rockeries, laying stone paths, creating a delectable water garden. Like York Cottage, the Moulin contained a profusion of trite mottoes. Many of them were embroidered on cushions and the duchess had a particular favourite: 'You Can Never Be Too Rich or Too Thin.'

Their Neuilly mansion, though known as the Villa Windsor, was a palace in all but name. Guarded by a lodge and enormous iron gates crowned with gilded spikes, it was approached along a sweeping gravel drive flanked by lawns, oak and chestnut trees and clumps of rhododendrons. A colonnaded portico led into a grand foyer dominated by a silken banner emblazoned with the Prince of Wales's coat of arms hanging from a second-floor gallery, above which rose a sky-blue vault painted with fluffy clouds and flying geese and framed by a *trompe l'oeil* balustrade. In the centre of the marble floor, surrounded by octagonal mirrors, porcelain vases, crystal girandoles, Regency-style consoles supported by gilt eagles, and tiers of orchids and lilies, with an oriental screen in one corner and a sedan chair in the other, stood an ormolu and mahogany desk bearing the leather-bound visitors' book, a green velvet obelisk set with royal medallions and a red dispatch box inscribed in letters of gold, 'The King'. The salons leading off this hall were just as ornate, since the aim of the duchess's interior designer, Stéphane Boudin, was to create 'an Italian palazzo in the rococo style'.[17] Amid eighteenth-century French furniture and regal portraiture was a gleaming array of priceless bric-à-brac – jade elephants, Meissen pugs, Lalique goblets, Sèvres figurines, lacquered caskets, alabaster urns, Georgian silver, bloodstone seals, gold timepieces, jewelled boxes. The food was equally sumptuous, though the Windsors ate like birds. And thanks to the duchess's meticulous, almost neurotic, attention to detail, the large staff provided immaculate service. 'I married a bell pusher,' she told Anne Seagrim, 'so I have to make sure there is someone to answer the bell.' All told, the duke's last home provided him with a fantastic simulacrum of majesty.

In 1951 he was 'tickled pink' when the Windsors were elected 'America's Happiest Married Couple'.[18] Yet ironically the early years of this decade saw the lowest point in their marriage. This was because the duchess embarked on a reckless flirtation with Jimmy Donahue, who was not only gay, in both senses of the word, but grossly extravagant – in a Paris nightclub he once bought her a 'jeroboam of scent'.[19] Perhaps she felt suffocated by the duke's dogged adoration or trapped by having to compensate for all he had sacrificed on her account. Or maybe, as some inferred, she had never truly loved him and gained some satisfaction from indulging his taste for humiliation. Certainly the duchess enjoyed camp company and the duke did not, though for a time he seemed to be amused by Donahue's inane antics and salacious wit. In three successive summers the trio went on Mediterranean cruises, paid for with Woolworth money. The duke also accepted personal gifts from Donahue and at one of his parties Edward allowed himself to be photographed with Wallis, both wearing elaborate paper crowns. But as the duchess dined, danced and canoodled with her new consort, whose private life was a miasma of drugs and orgies, the duke became increasingly miserable. Often the association, which generated garish publicity, reduced him to tears. Yet when an old friend tried to intervene the duke responded, 'Anything that makes Wallis happy is okay with me.'[20] In 1954, however, she fell out with Donahue and the duke banished their court jester, who explained his dismissal by saying: 'I've abdicated.'[21]

When filling out an application form for a Florida driving licence, the duke wrote in the box marked Occupation: 'None'. Lord Dudley persuaded him to change this to 'Peer of the Realm', but the first answer was essentially correct. For all practical purposes the duke's last years were empty, idle and aimless. As well as smoking, golfing and gardening, he kept boredom at bay by attending to the retinue of pugs while his wife was closeted with couturiers, coiffeuses, manicuristes, masseuses and, of course, domestiques. Dressing and undressing also gave him something to do and he even produced a final, heavily ghosted book that was largely about clothes, *A Family Album* (1960). However he did have one serious preoccupation: lucre. He played both the stock market and the black market, engaging in illegal currency dealings which netted him, according to his secretary Victor Waddilove, 'well over £200,000'.[22] Unhappily for the duke, Waddilove defrauded him of substantial sums in the course of these transactions. When exposed in 1958, the secretary averted prosecution by threatening to implicate the duke, who, advised by Walter Monckton and others, paid him hush money.

The Windsors' fortune was hardly dented and they continued to travel in state and to dispense lavish hospitality. But their guests, who included patricians and plutocrats such as Sir Oswald Mosley, were unkindly described as a 'weird collection of social derelicts'.[23] And far from being feasts of reason, their dinner parties culminated in games, dancing, sing-songs or charades. Wallis once made her husband dress up in a tutu and a blonde wig and dance *Swan Lake*. The lighter the entertainment the more they enjoyed it, the duke once exclaiming: 'Isn't "The King and I" a wonderful show?'[24] Lacking intellectual interests, the Windsors did jigsaw puzzles. She dabbled in astrology while he engaged in a more refined form of superstition, genealogy. Increasingly the duke echoed the opinions of the extreme right, asserting that the Second World War was mainly caused by 'Roosevelt and the Jews'.[25] Noël Coward thought him 'completely idiotic'.[26] Cecil Beaton said that he resembled 'a mad terrier'.[27] Others found him vacuous and pathetic. Even Anne Seagrim, who admired the Windsors despite their cavalier treatment of her, acknowledged that 'their life together was one of loneliness and waste'.[28]

Lord Mountbatten warned Prince Charles against the kind of self-indulgence that had ruined his great-uncle, leading to 'his disgraceful Abdication and his futile life ever after'.[29]

Nevertheless, as the duke aged he remained popular in England. Basking in a glow of nostalgia, he was applauded by London theatre-goers. Even when the past returned to haunt him, it did little or no damage to his standing. In 1957 German documents about his role in the Second World War were published and, although Churchill's government had wanted to suppress them, they were easily dismissed as self-serving misrepresentations. The duke was more annoyed by the Palace's refusal to let him see sections concerning himself in Sir John Wheeler-Bennett's official biography of George VI, a discourtesy for which he blamed 'that evil snake Lascelles'.[30] Eventually, after threatening legal action, he was permitted to examine the text and make corrections; anyway the book, which appeared in 1958, was predictably anodyne.

In that year the duke suffered from a debilitating attack of shingles, which left him a shadow of his former self. During the next decade his health deteriorated, as did his hearing and his short-term memory. In 1964 he underwent open heart surgery; in 1965 he had a major eye operation; in 1968 he was treated for an arthritic hip. As he began to fail, there was a slight thaw in his relationship with the royal family. In 1967 Queen Elizabeth II invited both him and the duchess to attend the dedication of a plaque outside Marlborough House commemorating Queen Mary. In

1970, having decided against Baltimore as his last resting place, he got approval to be buried, along with his wife, in the royal necropolis at Frogmore.

In 1971 the duke was diagnosed with throat cancer. He endured the affliction and the treatment with his usual courage. When the queen visited him shortly before the end, he insisted on standing and bowing to her, even at the risk of detaching the tube connecting him to a drip. The duke died on 28 May 1972. Sixty thousand mourners filed past his coffin as he lay in state at St George's Chapel, Windsor. Attending the funeral, the frail and bewildered duchess stayed with the queen. Subsequently she sank into a tragic state of senility, dying in 1986.

Noël Coward had remarked that, in gratitude for removing Edward VIII from the throne and the country, 'a statue to Mrs Simpson should be erected on every village green'.[31] Many who saw the king's short reign from close quarters might have sympathized with this sentiment, though it would not have appealed to most of his subjects, who had long been captivated by the legend and the life of Prince Charming. The fact is, though, that his conduct on becoming king was so irresponsible that it undermined the trust of courtiers and ministers. More, it demonstrated the perennial wisdom of Walter Bagehot's warning (which referred to Edward VII) about the danger of having, 'upon a constitutional throne, an active and meddling fool'.[32] To be sure, Edward, who prided himself on being a modern man, was understandably reluctant to become a monarchical marionette – whereas George VI's willingness to go through the appropriate motions made his reign a comparative success. But Edward's infatuation with Wallis drove out whatever sense his crown might have encompassed.

Time and again witnesses said that they had never seen one 'human being so utterly and completely possessed by another as he was by her'.[33] To marry her he happily renounced his heritage and, resolutely faithful, he never seemed to regret it. But his abdication traumatized the monarchy. It weakened the tenure of its existence in a fledgling democracy, for if a king could quit on a whim the sovereign people might aspire to elect their head of state. It so lacerated the royal family that the truth had to be suppressed, only to seep out drop by toxic drop. Edward was ahead of his time in rejecting the stigma of divorce, but his successors felt bound to maintain the sanctity of marriage, to the detriment of Queen Elizabeth's sister and her eldest son. Above all the abdication crisis revealed the fundamental flaw in the system of hereditary succession, namely that accident of birth is liable to bestow the crown on someone quite unfit to wear it. Some people said that Edward was a victim of fate but he denied this, declaring with characteristic candour that 'the fault lay not in my stars but in my genes'.[34]

# Notes

## I. ROYAL DESTINY

1. F. Donaldson, *Edward VIII* (London: Weidenfeld & Nicolson, 1986), p. 7.
2. K. Middlemas and J. Barnes, *Baldwin: A Biography* (London: Weidenfeld & Nicolson, 1969), p. 976.
3. *Review of Reviews* XVI (July 1897), p. 85.
4. J. Pope-Hennessy, *Queen Mary* (London: Allen & Unwin, 1959), p. 258. The phrase was that of Queen Victoria's eldest child, Empress Frederick of Germany.
5. M. Bloch, *The Secret File of the Duke of Windsor* (London: Corgi, 1989), p. 327.
6. K. Rose, *George V* (London: Weidenfeld & Nicolson, 1983), p. 303.
7. Duke of Windsor, *A King's Story* (London: Prion, 1998), p. 59.
8. Ibid., p. 78.
9. K. O. Morgan (ed.), *Lloyd George: Family Letters 1885–1936* (Cardiff: University of Wales Press, 1973), p. 159.
10. Duke of Windsor, *King's Story*, p. 79.
11. K. Rose, *Kings, Queens and Courtiers* (London: Weidenfeld & Nicolson, 1985), p. 73.
12. R. Rhodes James (ed.), *Memoirs of a Conservative* (London: Weidenfeld & Nicolson, 1969), p. 19.
13. H. Bolitho, *King Edward VIII: His Life and Reign* (London: Eyre and Spottiswoode, 1937), p. 37.
14. G. Dennis, *Coronation Commentary* (London: Heinemann, 1937), p. 220.
15. Duke of Windsor, *A Family Album* (London: Cassell, 1960), p. 45.
16. R. McKibbin, *Classes and Cultures: England 1918–1951* (Oxford: Oxford University Press, 2000 edn), p. 4.
17. Bolitho, *Edward VIII*, p. 45.
18. Duke of Windsor, *King's Story*, p. 102.
19. M. Bostridge, *The Fateful Year: England 1914* (London: Viking, 2014), p. 273.
20. P. Magnus, *King Edward the Seventh* (Harmondsworth: Penguin, 1967), p. 78.
21. Duke of Windsor, *King's Story*, p. 121.
22. R. Godfrey (ed.), *Letters from a Prince* (London: Little, Brown, 1998), pp. 36, 30 and 96.
23. J. Lees-Milne, *The Enigmatic Edwardian: The Life of Reginald, 2nd Viscount Esher* (London: Sidgwick & Jackson, 1986), pp. 300 and 160.
24. Countess of Airlie, *Thatched with Gold* (Leicester: Ulverscroft, 1962), p. 146.
25. Godfrey, *Letters from a Prince*, pp. 115 and 156.

## 2. PRINCE IMPERIAL

1. P. Ziegler, *King Edward VIII: The Official Biography* (London: Collins, 1990), p. 89.
2. Rhodes James, *Memoirs of a Conservative*, p. 55.
3. Godfrey, *Letters from a Prince*, pp. 94, 329, 169, 232 and 144.
4. F. Giles, *Sundry Times* (London: Murray, 1986), p. 24.
5. J. Bryan III and C. J. V. Murphy, *The Windsor Story* (London: Granada, 1979), p. 84.
6. Godfrey, *Letters from a Prince*, pp. 228, 128 and 289.
7. D. Judd, *George VI* (London: Michael Joseph, 1982), p. 71.
8. Duke of Windsor, *King's Story*, pp. 123–4 and 143.
9. P. Brendon and P. Whitehead, *The Windsors: A Dynasty Revealed* (London: Hodder & Stoughton, 1994), p. 36. This letter was written on Christmas Day 1919.
10. Ziegler, *Edward VIII*, p. 124.
11. P. Ziegler (ed.), *The Diaries of Lord Louis Mountbatten 1920–1922* (London: Collins, 1987), p. 137.
12. Godfrey, *Letters from a Prince*, p. 348.
13. W. Shawcross, *Queen Elizabeth The Queen Mother* (London: Macmillan, 2009), p. 409.
14. D. Hart-Davis (ed.), *In Royal Service: The Letters and Journals of Sir Alan Lascelles 1920–1936*, II (London: Hamish Hamilton, 1989), p. 15.
15. F. Prochaska, *Royal Bounty: The Making of a Welfare Monarchy* (London: Yale University Press, 1995), p. 201.
16. P. Hall, *Royal Fortune: Tax, Money & the Monarchy* (London: Bloomsbury, 1992), p. 56.
17. Duke of Windsor, *King's Story*, p. 63.
18. Ziegler (ed.), *Diaries of Lord Louis Mountbatten*, p. 239.
19. H. Russell, *With the Prince in the East* (London: Methuen, 1922), p. 135.
20. Hart-Davis (ed.), *In Royal Service*, p. 65.
21. Bryan and Murphy, *Windsor Story*, p. 58.
22. Hart-Davis (ed.), *In Royal Service*, p. 48.
23. R. Hyam, *Britain's Declining Empire: The Road to Decolonisation 1918–1968* (Cambridge: Cambridge University Press, 2006), p. 70.
24. Pope-Hennessy, *Queen Mary*, p. 516.
25. J. Morgan, *Edwina Mountbatten: A Life of Her Own* (London: HarperCollins, 1991), p. 105.
26. Hart-Davis (ed.), *In Royal Service*, p. 50.
27. E. Trzebinski, *The Lives of Beryl Markham* (London: Heinemann, 1993), p. 130.
28. C[hurchill] A[rchives] C[entre], GBR/0014/BREN, interview with John Grigg. The governor was the prince's former adviser, Edward Grigg.
29. S. Bradford, *King George VI* (London: Weidenfeld & Nicolson, 1989), p. 229.
30. Hart-Davis (ed.), *In Royal Service*, p. 120.

## 3. PUBLIC FIGURE, PRIVATE LIFE

1. Ziegler, *Edward VIII*, p. 164.
2. Magnus, *Edward the Seventh*, p. 477.

3. R. Rhodes James (ed.), *Chips: The Diaries of Sir Henry Channon* (London: Weidenfeld & Nicolson, 1967), p. 77.

4. C. Stuart (ed.), *The Reith Diaries* (London: Collins, 1975), p. 184.

5. A. Olechnowicz (ed.), *The Monarchy and the British Nation, 1780 to the Present* (Cambridge: Cambridge University Press, 2007), p. 261.

6. G. Vanderbilt and Thelma Lady Furness, *Double Exposure: A Twin Autobiography* (London: F. Muller, 1959), p. 266.

7. *Documents on German Foreign Policy 1918–1945* Series C, IV (London: HMSO, 1962), p. 49.

8. Rhodes James (ed.), *Chips*, p. 84.

9. *Evening Standard*, 17 April 1933.

10. C. Mackenzie, *The Windsor Tapestry* (London: Rich & Cowan, 1938), p. 217.

11. Duchess of Windsor, *The Heart Has Its Reasons* (London: Michael Joseph, 1956), p. 107.

12. A. Sebba, *That Woman: The Life of Wallis Simpson, Duchess of Windsor* (London: Weidenfeld & Nicolson, 2011), p. 55.

13. M. Bloch (ed.), *Wallis & Edward: Letters 1931–1937: The Intimate Correspondence of the Duke and Duchess of Windsor* (London: Weidenfeld & Nicolson, 1986), p. 11.

14. H. Vickers, *Cecil Beaton* (London: Weidenfeld & Nicolson, 1985), p. 193.

15. Bryan and Murphy, *Windsor Story*, p. 106.

16. J. J. Norwich (ed.), *The Duff Cooper Diaries 1915–1951* (London: Weidenfeld & Nicolson, 2005), p. 228.

17. A. Howard, *RAB: The Life of R. A. Butler* (London: Jonathan Cape, 1987), p. 66.

18. Bloch (ed.), *Wallis & Edward*, p. 89.

19. Duchess of Windsor, *Heart Has Its Reasons*, p. 197.

20. Sebba, *That Woman*, p. 100.

21. Bloch (ed.), *Wallis & Edward*, pp. 139 and 119–20.

22. F. Watson, 'The Death of George V' in *History Today* (December, 1986), p. 28.

23. H. Hardinge, *Loyal to Three Kings* (London: William Kimber, 1967), p. 61.

24. Judd, *George VI*, p. 125.

25. Donaldson, *Edward VIII*, p. 181.

# 4. KING EDWARD'S REIGN

1. P. Gibbs, *Ordeal in England* (London: Heinemann, 1938), p. 23.

2. CAC, CHAR 1/254/19, Churchill to Edward VIII, 2 February 1936.

3. Mackenzie, *Windsor Tapestry*, p. 148.

4. *Daily Herald*, 23 January 1936.

5. *Spectator*, 24 January 1936.

6. *Daily Mail*, 28 January 1936.

7. *Documents on German Foreign Policy 1918–1945*, Series C, IV, p. 1063. Like other German emissaries, the Duke of Coburg was anxious to inflate his own importance and cannot be relied on as a witness; but the new king's statement seems authentic.

8. Duke of Windsor, *King's Story*, p. 280.

9. Hardinge, *Loyal to Three Kings*, p. 76

10. M. Secrest, *Kenneth Clark* (London: Weidenfeld & Nicolson, 1984), p. 117.

11. H. Nicolson, *Diaries and Letters 1930–1939*, ed. by N. Nicolson (London: Collins, 1966), p. 232.

12. Rhodes James (ed.), *Chips*, p. 51.

13. J. G. Lockhart, *Cosmo Gordon Lang* (London: Hodder & Stoughton, 1949), p. 395.

14. Lord Harewood, *The Tongs and the Bones* (London: Weidenfeld & Nicolson, 1981), p. 17.

15. *Documents on German Foreign Policy 1918–1945*, Series C, V (1966), p. 193.

16. R. Rhodes James, *Victor Cazalet: A Portrait* (London: Hamish Hamilton, 1976), p. 209.

17. K. Young (ed.), *The Diaries of Sir Robert Bruce Lockhart* I (London: Macmillan, 1973), p. 340. The Russian ambassador, Ivan Maisky, who penned a detailed account of the interview, said that Litvinov thought the king 'a lively and spirited man'. (G. Gorodetsky [ed.], *The Maisky Diaries* [London: Yale University Press, 2015], p. 64.)

18. R. A. Jones, *Arthur Ponsonby: The Politics of Life* (Bromley: Helm, 1989), p. 217.

19. Hall, *Royal Fortune*, p. 70.

20. Hardinge, *Loyal to Three Kings*, p. 84.

21. Bradford, *George VI*, p. 172.

22. Bloch (ed.), *Wallis & Edward*, p. 173.

23. S. Williams, *The People's King: The True Story of the Abdication* (London: Allen Lane, 2003), p. 96.

24. Bloch (ed.), *Wallis & Edward*, p. 139.

25. Lord Birkenhead, *Lord Monckton* (London: Weidenfeld & Nicolson, 1969), p. 128.

26. S. Menkes, *The Windsor Style* (London: Grafton, 1987), p. 139.

27. *Daily Mail*, 23 July 2010,

28. Bloch (ed.), *Wallis & Edward*, pp. 194 and 196.

29. CAC, GBR/0014/BREN, interview with Lord Hardinge.

30. Duchess of Windsor, *Heart Has Its Reasons*, p. 230.

31. R. Rhodes James, *A Spirit Undaunted: The Political Role of George VI* (London: Little, Brown, 1998), p. 109.

32. Lord Beaverbrook, *The Abdication of King Edward VIII*, ed. by A. J. P. Taylor (London: Hamish Hamilton, 1966), p. 30.

33. *New York Times*, 18 October 1936.

34. Norwich (ed.), *Duff Cooper Diaries*, p. 226.

35. Donaldson, *Edward VIII*, p. 230.

36. Viscount Templewood, *Nine Troubled Years* (London: Collins, 1954), p. 219.

37. *Daily Herald*, 20 November 1936.

38. Rhodes James (ed.), *Chips*, pp. 83–4.

39. A. Lascelles, *King's Counsellor: Abdication and War*, ed. by D. Hart-Davis (London: Weidenfeld & Nicolson, 2006), p. 108.

40. D. Duff, *Queen Mary* (London: Collins, 1985), p. 208.

41. Donaldson, *Edward VIII*, p. 274.

42. M. Bloch, *The Reign and Abdication of Edward VIII* (London: Bantam, 1990), p. 92.

43. *The Times*, 3 December 1936.

44. Beaverbrook, *Abdication*, p. 102.

45. Duchess of Windsor, *Heart Has Its Reasons*, p. 256.

46. A. J. P. Taylor, *Beaverbrook* (London: Hamish Hamilton, 1972), p. 370.

47. *The Times*, 8 December 1936.

48. Rhodes James (ed.), *Chips*, p. 97.

49. W. Churchill, 'King Edward VIII' in *Great Contemporaries*, ed. by J. W. Muller (Wilmington, Del.: ISI Books, 2012), p. 416.

50. Duke of Windsor, *King's Story*, p. 413.

## 5. THE DUKE OF WINDSOR AT BAY

1. *The Times*, 14 December 1936. A tacit but more pointed barb was the omission of 'Defender of the Faith' from the list of Edward's titles in the abdication legislation.

2. Birkenhead, *Monckton*, p. 154.

3. H. Jennings and C. Madge, *May the Twelfth 1937* (London: Faber & Faber, 1938), p. 303.

4. A. Lownie, *John Buchan: The Presbyterian Cavalier* (London: Pimlico, 2002), p. 258.

5. Lascelles, *King's Counsellor*, p. 415.

6. CAC, GBR/0014/BREN, interview with Nigel Nicolson.

7. E. F. Braley (ed.), *Letters of Herbert Hensley Henson* (London: SPCK, 1950), p. 99.

8. *Nation*, 19 December 1936.

9. M. Gilbert, *Winston S. Churchill, V, 1922–1939* (London: Heinemann, 1976), p. 823.

10. A. J. Sylvester, *Life with Lloyd George* (London: Macmillan, 1975), p. 193.

11. O. H. Bullitt (ed.), *For the President Personal and Secret: Correspondence between Franklin D. Roosevelt and William C. Bullitt* (London: Deutsch, 1973), p. 310.

12. A. Roberts, *Eminent Churchillians* (London: Simon & Schuster, 1994), p. 46.

13. *New York Times*, 17 January 1937.

14. Mackenzie, *Windsor Tapestry*, p. 566.

15. Bryan and Murphy, *Windsor Story*, p. 314.

16. *New York Times*, 10 October 1937.

17. Bloch (ed.), *Wallis & Edward*, p. 233.

18. CAC, CHAR 2/300/39, Churchill to the Duke of Windsor, 17 May 1937.

19. Parliamentary Archives, BBK/C/86.

20. Gilbert, *Churchill V*, p. 810.

21. J. Vincent (ed.), *The Crawford Papers: The Journals of David Lindsay . . . 1892–1940* (Manchester: Manchester University Press, 1984), p. 617.

22. Ibid., p. 585.

23. CAC, CHAR 2/300/49, Churchill to the Duke of Windsor, 28 October 1937.

24. Bryan and Murphy, *Windsor Story*, p. 364.

25. *New York Times*, 7 November and 10 October 1937.

26. D. W. Hood, *Working for the Windsors* (London: A. Wingate, 1957), p. 113.

27. Ziegler, *Edward VIII*, p. 370.

28. CAC, CHAR 2/300/54, Monckton to Churchill, 5 December 1937.

29. Brendon and Whitehead, *The Windsors*, p. 103.

30. Vincent (ed.), *Crawford Papers*, p. 618.
31. T. Brown, *The Diana Chronicles* (London: Arrow, 2007), p. 89.
32. Bloch, *Secret File*, p. 173.
33. J. W. Wheeler-Bennett, *King George VI* (London: Macmillan, 1958), p. 348.
34. CAC, GBR/0014/BREN, interview with Frank Giles.
35. Donaldson, *Edward VIII*, p. 346.
36. Rhodes James, *Spirit Undaunted*, p. 175.
37. Vincent (ed.), *Crawford Papers*, p. 604.
38. Duchess of Windsor, *Heart Has Its Reasons*, p. 329.
39. CAC, CHAR 19/2A/86, Churchill to Duke of Windsor, 17 November 1939.
40. M. Bloch, *The Duke of Windsor's War* (London: Weidenfeld & Nicolson, 1982), p. 51.
41. CAC, CHAR 20/9A/16, Hoare to Churchill, 28 June 1940.
42. M. Bloch, *Operation Willi: The Plot to Kidnap the Duke of Windsor, July 1940* (London: Weidenfeld & Nicolson, 1984), pp. 91, 90 and 133.
43. CAC, CHAR 20/9B/120–22, Lord Lloyd message to Churchill, 20 July 1940.
44. M. Gilbert, *Winston S. Churchill* VI, *1939–1941* (London: Heinemann, 1983), p. 703.
45. Ibid., p. 700.
46. Rhodes James, *Spirit Undaunted*, p. 219.
47. Bloch, *Operation Willi*, p. 174.
48. CAC, CHAR 20/9B/146, Duke of Windsor to Churchill, 31 July 1940.

# 6. GOVERNOR OF THE BAHAMAS

1. CAC, CHAR 20/9B/180–81, Duke of Windsor to Lloyd, 26 August 1940.
2. CAC, CHAR 20/9B/182–5, Lloyd to Duke of Windsor, 27–9 August 1940.
3. Bloch, *Duke of Windsor's War*, pp. 148, 128 and 241.
4. CAC, CHAR 20/9A/93, Duke of Windsor to Churchill, 30 June 1941.
5. CAC, GBR/0014/BREN, interview with Frank Giles.
6. R. Forbes, *Appointment with Destiny* (London: Cassell, 1946), pp. 208 and 143.
7. E. Dupuch, *Tribune Story* (London: Benn, 1967), p. 90.
8. CAC, CHAR 20/63/72–4, Duke of Windsor to Churchill, 10 November 1942.
9. CAC, CHAR 20/31A/3. Harry Hopkins used these words to Churchill.
10. CAC, CHAR 20/31A/70, Frazier Jelke, 17 April 1941.
11. CAC, CHAR 20/31A/140, Churchill to Duke of Windsor, 13 September 1941.
12. CAC, CHAR 20/31A/16, 17 March 1941.
13. *Sunday Dispatch*, 16 March 1941.
14. CAC, CHAR 20/31A/12, 11 March 1941.
15. CAC, CHAR 20/31A/50, Halifax to Churchill, 27 March 1941.
16. CAC, CHAR 20/31A/30, Churchill to Duke of Windsor, 20 March 1941.
17. CAC, CHAR 20/31A/51, Duke of Windsor to Churchill, 27 March 1941.
18. CAC, CHAR 20/31A/93, Duke of Windsor to Churchill, 30 June 1941.
19. CAC, CHAR 20/31B/156, Churchill to Duke of Windsor, 22 September 1941.
20. R. MacColl, *Deadline and Dateline* (London: Oldbourne Press, 1956), pp. 128 and 131.
21. CAC, CHAR 20/31B/161–2, Halifax to Churchill, 19 October 1941.

22. CAC, CHAR 20/63/75, Duke of Windsor to Churchill, 10 November 1942.

23. M. Pye, *The King Over the Water* (London: Hutchinson, 1981), p. 176.

24. M. Craton and G. Saunders, *Islanders in the Stream: A History of the Bahamian People* II (Athens, Ga.: University of Georgia Press, 1998), p. 292.

25. Pye, *King Over the Water*, p. 239.

26. A. de Marigny with M. Herskowitz, *A Conspiracy of Crowns: The True Story of the Duke of Windsor and the Murder of Sir Harry Oakes* (London: Bantam, 1990), p. 299.

27. Bloch, *Secret File*, p. 253.

28. CAC, CHAR 20/63/92, Churchill to Duke of Windsor, 22 December 1942.

29. Bloch, *Secret File*, p. 255.

30. Lascelles, *King's Counsellor*, p. 223.

31. D. Cadbury, *Princes at War: The British Royal Family's Private Battle in the Second World War* (London: Bloomsbury, 2015), p. 329.

# 7. LAST YEARS

1. CAC, SEAG 1/1/1, Anne Seagrim, 8 September 1950.

2. S. M. Alsop, *To Marietta from Paris* (London: Weidenfeld & Nicolson, 1976), p. 80.

3. CAC, GBR/0014/BREN, interview with Barbara Cartland.

4. Sebba, *That Woman*, p. 255.

5. CAC, SEAG 1/1/10, Anne Seagrim, 21 November 1950.

6. CAC CHUR 2/178/117, Bracken to Churchill, 17 July 1950.

7. CAC, CHUR 2/178/153, Churchill to George VI, 18 November 1945.

8. Ziegler, *Edward VIII*, pp. 531–2.

9. CAC, SEAG 1/1/29, Anne Seagrim, 1 May 1951.

10. Shawcross, *Queen Elizabeth*, p. 660.

11. Bloch, *Secret File*, p. 308.

12. M. Thornton, *Royal Feud: The Queen Mother and the Duchess of Windsor* (London: Macmillan, 1985), pp. 257–8.

13. Bloch, *Secret File*, pp. 312, 319, 324 and 329.

14. CAC, SEAG 1/2/26, Anne Seagrim, 6 March 1953.

15. Duke of Windsor, *The Crown and the People 1902–1953* (London: Cassell, 1953), p. 8.

16. P. Quennell (ed.), *A Lonely Business: A Self-Portrait of James Pope-Hennessy* (London: Weidenfeld & Nicolson, 1981), p. 211.

17. G. King, *The Duchess of Windsor* (London: Aurum, 1999), pp. 407 and 404.

18. CAC, SEAG 1/6 and 1/2/11, Anne Seagrim to Joan Ingram, 19 December 1951.

19. C. Wilson, *Dancing with the Devil* (London: HarperCollins, 2000), p. 9.

20. Bryan and Murphy, *Windsor Story*, p. 481.

21. Wilson, *Dancing with the Devil*, p. 219.

22. Roberts, *Eminent Churchillians*, p. 280.

23. C. L. Sulzberger, *A Long Row of Candles* (London: Macdonald, 1969), p. 599.

24. CAC, SEAG 1/3, 25 January 1952.

25. Giles, *Sundry Times*, p. 131.

26. G. Payn and S. Morley (eds), *The Noël Coward Diaries* (London: Weidenfeld & Nicolson, 1982), p. 323.
27. Vickers, *Beaton*, p. 459.
28. CAC, SEAG 1/6.
29. P. Ziegler, *Mountbatten: The Official Biography* (London: Fontana, 1986), p. 686.
30. Bloch, *Secret File*, p. 347.
31. S. Morley, *Noël Coward* (London: Haus, 2005), p. 63.
32. W. Bagehot, *The English Constitution* (London: C. A. Watts, 1964), p. 119.
33. CAC, GBR/0014/BREN, interview with Sir Kenneth de Courcy.
34. Duke of Windsor, *King's Story*, p. 284.

# Further Reading

Of the making of books about the Windsors there is no end. Many of them do not even strive to be objective and what the duke and duchess wrote about themselves, with ghostly assistance, is especially self-serving. It is nonetheless indispensable. The duke's memoir *A King's Story* (London: Cassell, 1951, reissued by Prion, 1998) is lucid, detailed and well written. His other books also repay examination: *The Crown and the People 1902–1953* (London: Cassell, 1953) and *A Family Album* (London: Cassell, 1960). The Duchess of Windsor's *The Heart Has Its Reasons* (London: Michael Joseph, 1956) is surprisingly candid in places. Much more revealing, though, are Edward's callow missives to his first mistress, Freda Dudley Ward, edited by R. Godfrey: *Letters from a Prince* (London: Little, Brown, 1998).

Alan Lascelles provided a first-hand and often acerbic view of Edward as prince, king and duke in two volumes, both edited by Duff Hart-Davis: *In Royal Service: The Letters and Journals of Sir Alan Lascelles 1920–1936* (London: Hamish Hamilton, 1989); and *King's Counsellor: Abdication and War* (London: Weidenfeld & Nicolson, 2006). Also acerbic was another royal private secretary, Alexander Hardinge, whose service to Edward VIII is vividly described by his wife Helen in *Loyal to Three Kings* (London: Kimber, 1967). Authentic glimpses of the Prince of Wales on tour appear in *The Diaries of Lord Louis Mountbatten 1920–1922*, edited by Philip Ziegler (London: Collins, 1987). Similarly *Chips: The Diaries of Sir Henry Channon*, edited by Robert Rhodes James (London: Weidenfeld & Nicolson, 1967), gives an intimate portrait of King

Edward and Mrs Simpson during the abdication crisis. A less sympathetic but equally graphic picture emerges from *The Windsor Story* (London: Granada, 1979), by J. Bryan III and C. J. V. Murphy.

The best life of the monarch is Philip Ziegler's official biography, *King Edward VIII* (London: Collins, 1990). It is judicious, comprehensive and based on thorough research, especially in the Royal Archives, an institution wedded to secrecy. If Ziegler is consistently respectful, Frances Donaldson's excellent *Edward VIII* (London: Weidenfeld & Nicolson, 1974, reissued 1986) is sharply critical. It superseded earlier works, which nevertheless contain pertinent details, such as Hector Bolitho's laughably ambivalent *King Edward VIII: His Life and Reign* (London: Eyre and Spottiswoode, 1937) and Compton Mackenzie's indignant apologia, *The Windsor Tapestry* (London: Rich & Cowan, 1938). Michael Bloch was also a clear partisan of the Windsors but his volumes contain rich deposits of original material: *The Duke of Windsor's War* (London: Weidenfeld & Nicolson, 1982); and *Operation Willi: The Plot to Kidnap of Duke of Windsor, July 1940* (London: Weidenfeld & Nicolson, 1984); and *The Secret File of the Duke of Windsor* (London: Corgi, 1986); and *Wallis & Edward: Letters 1931–1937: The Intimate Correspondence of the Duke and Duchess of Windsor* (London: Weidenfeld & Nicolson, 1986).

Bloch has also written *The Reign and Abdication of Edward VIII* (London: Bantam, 1990), a shorter account of the event than Brian Inglis's *Abdication* (London: Hodder & Stoughton, 1966). These are improvements on Lord Beaverbrook's *The Abdication of King Edward VIII*, edited by A. J. P. Taylor (London: Hamish Hamilton, 1966), since the press baron was an interesting but all too interested party to the debacle and, although readable, he is characteristically unreliable. More recently, in *The People's King: The True Story of the Abdication* (London: Allen Lane, 2003), Susan Williams has provided piquant new data about the subject; but although her research was prodigious her conclusions are dubious.

The official biographies of King George V and Queen Mary give substantial but eminently discreet accounts of Edward VIII's family background: Harold Nicolson, *King George V: His Life and Reign* (London: Constable, 1952); and James Pope-Hennessy, *Queen Mary* (London: Allen & Unwin, 1959). These are helpfully supplemented by Kenneth Rose's *George V* (London: Weidenfeld & Nicolson, 1983) and David Duff's *Queen Mary* (London: Collins, 1985). Sir John Wheeler-Bennett's official life of Edward's brother, *King George VI* (London: Macmillan, 1958), is reticent even by the usual standards of the genre. Luckily Sarah Bradford's *King George VI* (London: Weidenfeld & Nicolson, 1989) is superb. Moreover Robert Rhodes James has compiled a useful pendant, *A Spirit Undaunted: The Political Role of George VI* (London: Little, Brown, 1998). William Shawcross's official life of Edward's sister-in-law, *Queen Elizabeth The Queen Mother* (London: Macmillan, 2009) is extremely long and full of inside information. But it omits almost everything to its subject's discredit, succumbing to the prevailing weakness of royal historical biographies – retrospective sycophancy.

The Windsors' protracted quarrel with the royal family has been covered in a number of books, including *The Windsors: A Dynasty Revealed* (London: Hodder & Stoughton, 1994), by Piers Brendon and Phillip Whitehead. But Michael Thornton's, *Royal Feud: The Queen Mother and the Duchess of Windsor* (London: Macmillan, 1985) was the groundbreaking work. It was followed by Kirsty McLeod's *Battle Royal: Edward VIII & George VI* (London: Constable, 1999) and Deborah Cadbury's *Princes at War: The British Royal Family's Private Battle in the Second World War* (London: Bloomsbury, 2015). Both tell a familiar story with verve but neither adds much of significance to it, and the latter conjures with conspiracy theories. Quite outstanding, though, is Phillip Hall's *Royal Fortune: Tax, Money & the Monarchy* (London: Bloomsbury, 1992), which unearths with rare incisiveness the financial roots of the brothers' mutual animosity. What the duke's money could buy is explored by Suzy Menkes in *The Royal Jewels* (London: Granada, 1985) and *The Windsor Style* (London: Grafton, 1987), and by Hugo Vickers in *The Private World of the Duke and Duchess of Windsor* (London: Harrods Publishing, 1995).

There is no entirely satisfactory biography of the Duchess of Windsor and some, such as Charles Higham's *Wallis: Secret Lives of the Duchess of Windsor* (London: Sidgwick & Jackson, 1988), are quite untrustworthy. Solid works are Ralph G. Martin's *The Woman He Loved* (London: W. H. Allen, 1974) and Greg King's *The Duchess of Windsor* (London: Aurum, 1999). More recently Anne Sebba has produced a fresh and lively, if sometimes speculative, portrayal: *That Woman: The Life of Wallis Simpson, Duchess of Windsor* (London: Weidenfeld & Nicolson, 2011).

The Windsors have also inspired quite a few avowed works of fiction. Among the best are novels by William Boyd, *Any Human Heart* (London: Hamish Hamilton, 2002), and D. J. Taylor, *The Windsor Faction* (London: Chatto & Windus, 2013); and the title tale in Rose Tremain's collection of short stories, *The Darkness of Wallis Simpson* (London: Chatto & Windus, 2005).

# Picture Credits

1. Queen Victoria with the future Kings George V, Edward VII and Edward VIII, 1899 (Mary Evans Picture Library/Alamy)
2. The Prince of Wales's investiture at Caernarfon, 1911 (Getty Images)
3. Edward with the Black Watch, 1918 (AP/PA Photos)
4. Edward in Launceston, Australia, 1920 (National Archives of Australia, Canberra, A1861:4538)
5. Sir William Orpen, *The Prince of Wales as Captain of the Royal & Ancient Golf Club, St Andrews in 1922*, 1927 (The Royal & Ancient Golf Club/Bridgeman Images)
6. Freda Dudley Ward, 1918 (Illustrated London News Ltd/Mary Evans)
7. Edward with Thelma Furness, 1932 (Getty Images)
8. Edward with Mrs Simpson, Dalmatian coast, 1936 (Getty Images)
9. Edward at Boverton, Glamorgan, 18 November 1936 (Getty Images)
10. Postcard commemorating the 'Year of the Three Kings', 1936 (Getty Images)
11. The Windsors' wedding, front cover of the French newspaper supplement *L'illustré du petit Journal*, 13 June 1937 (Getty Images)
12. Edward visiting Adolf Hitler at the Berghof, Obersalzberg (Mary Evans/Süddeutsche Zeitung Photo)
13. The Windsors in Madrid, June 1940 (Getty Images)
14. Flamingo brooch made for the duchess by Cartier, 1940 (Rex Features/Sotheby's)

# Acknowledgements

I am grateful to the Sir Winston Churchill Archive Trust for permission to quote from the papers of Sir Winston, which are housed at the Churchill Archives Centre in Cambridge. This has enabled me to illustrate in telling detail Churchill's important relationship with the subject of this biography. I must also thank the Master and Fellows of Churchill College for permission to quote from the newly available papers of Anne Seagrim, whose copyright is vested in them. As always, I much appreciate the generous assistance and expert guidance of the Archive Centre's staff. Its Director Allen Packwood was especially helpful, as were Natalie Adams and Katharine Thomson. Simon Gough at the Parliamentary Archives gave additional help. I am greatly indebted to the brilliant team at Penguin who made the publication of this book so trouble-free and so pleasurable: Linden Lawson, Cecilia Mackay, Alan Rutter, Anna Hervé, and Stuart Proffitt, who not only commissioned it but contributed valuable suggestions for its improvement. A slim volume can be harder to write than a fat one and in this endeavour I have benefited more than I can say from the aid, encouragement and support of my wife, Vyvyen.

# Index

# *Penguin Monarchs*

## THE HOUSES OF WESSEX AND DENMARK

| | |
|---|---|
| Athelstan* | Tom Holland |
| Aethelred the Unready | Richard Abels |
| Cnut | Ryan Lavelle |
| Edward the Confessor | |

## THE HOUSES OF NORMANDY, BLOIS AND ANJOU

| | |
|---|---|
| William I* | Marc Morris |
| William II | John Gillingham |
| Henry I | Edmund King |
| Stephen | Carl Watkins |
| Henry II* | Richard Barber |
| Richard I | Thomas Asbridge |
| John | Nicholas Vincent |

## THE HOUSE OF PLANTAGENET

| | |
|---|---|
| Henry III | Stephen Church |
| Edward I* | Andy King |
| Edward II | Christopher Given-Wilson |
| Edward III* | Jonathan Sumption |
| Richard II* | Laura Ashe |

## THE HOUSES OF LANCASTER AND YORK

| | |
|---|---|
| Henry IV | Catherine Nall |
| Henry V* | Anne Curry |
| Henry VI | James Ross |
| Edward IV | A. J. Pollard |
| Edward V | Thomas Penn |
| Richard III | Rosemary Horrox |

* Now in paperback

## THE HOUSE OF TUDOR

| | |
|---|---|
| Henry VII | Sean Cunningham |
| Henry VIII* | John Guy |
| Edward VI* | Stephen Alford |
| Mary I* | John Edwards |
| Elizabeth I | Helen Castor |

## THE HOUSE OF STUART

| | |
|---|---|
| James I | Thomas Cogswell |
| Charles I* | Mark Kishlansky |
| [Cromwell* | David Horspool] |
| Charles II* | Clare Jackson |
| James II | David Womersley |
| William III & Mary II* | Jonathan Keates |
| Anne | Richard Hewlings |

## THE HOUSE OF HANOVER

| | |
|---|---|
| George I | Tim Blanning |
| George II | Norman Davies |
| George III | Amanda Foreman |
| George IV | Stella Tillyard |
| William IV | Roger Knight |
| Victoria* | Jane Ridley |

## THE HOUSES OF SAXE-COBURG & GOTHA AND WINDSOR

| | |
|---|---|
| Edward VII* | Richard Davenport-Hines |
| George V* | David Cannadine |
| Edward VIII* | Piers Brendon |
| George VI* | Philip Ziegler |
| Elizabeth II* | Douglas Hurd |

\* Now in paperback

ALLEN LANE
*an imprint of*
PENGUIN BOOKS

# Also Published

Stephen Kotkin, *Stalin, Vol. II: Waiting for Hitler, 1928-1941*

Lindsey Fitzharris, *The Butchering Art: Joseph Lister's Quest to Transform the Grisly World of Victorian Medicine*

Serhii Plokhy, *Lost Kingdom: A History of Russian Nationalism from Ivan the Great to Vladimir Putin*

Mark Mazower, *What You Did Not Tell: A Russian Past and the Journey Home*

Lawrence Freedman, *The Future of War: A History*

Niall Ferguson, *The Square and the Tower: Networks, Hierarchies and the Struggle for Global Power*

Matthew Walker, *Why We Sleep: The New Science of Sleep and Dreams*

Edward O. Wilson, *The Origins of Creativity*

John Bradshaw, *The Animals Among Us: The New Science of Anthropology*

David Cannadine, *Victorious Century: The United Kingdom, 1800-1906*

Leonard Susskind and Art Friedman, *Special Relativity and Classical Field Theory*

Maria Alyokhina, *Riot Days*

Oona A. Hathaway and Scott J. Shapiro, *The Internationalists: And Their Plan to Outlaw War*

Chris Renwick, *Bread for All: The Origins of the Welfare State*

Anne Applebaum, *Red Famine: Stalin's War on Ukraine*

Richard McGregor, *Asia's Reckoning: The Struggle for Global Dominance*

Chris Kraus, *After Kathy Acker: A Biography*

Clair Wills, *Lovers and Strangers: An Immigrant History of Post-War Britain*

Odd Arne Westad, *The Cold War: A World History*

Max Tegmark, *Life 3.0: Being Human in the Age of Artificial Intelligence*

Jonathan Losos, *Improbable Destinies: How Predictable is Evolution?*

Chris D. Thomas, *Inheritors of the Earth: How Nature Is Thriving in an Age of Extinction*

Chris Patten, *First Confession: A Sort of Memoir*

James Delbourgo, *Collecting the World: The Life and Curiosity of Hans Sloane*

Naomi Klein, *No Is Not Enough: Defeating the New Shock Politics*

Ulrich Raulff, *Farewell to the Horse: The Final Century of Our Relationship*

Slavoj Žižek, *The Courage of Hopelessness: Chronicles of a Year of Acting Dangerously*

Patricia Lockwood, *Priestdaddy: A Memoir*

Ian Johnson, *The Souls of China: The Return of Religion After Mao*

Stephen Alford, *London's Triumph: Merchant Adventurers and the Tudor City*

Hugo Mercier and Dan Sperber, *The Enigma of Reason: A New Theory of Human Understanding*

Stuart Hall, *Familiar Stranger: A Life Between Two Islands*

Allen Ginsberg, *The Best Minds of My Generation: A Literary History of the Beats*

Sayeeda Warsi, *The Enemy Within: A Tale of Muslim Britain*

Alexander Betts and Paul Collier, *Refuge: Transforming a Broken Refugee System*

Robert Bickers, *Out of China: How the Chinese Ended the Era of Western Domination*

Erica Benner, *Be Like the Fox: Machiavelli's Lifelong Quest for Freedom*

William D. Cohan, *Why Wall Street Matters*

David Horspool, *Oliver Cromwell: The Protector*

Daniel C. Dennett, *From Bacteria to Bach and Back: The Evolution of Minds*

Derek Thompson, *Hit Makers: How Things Become Popular*

Harriet Harman, *A Woman's Work*

Wendell Berry, *The World-Ending Fire: The Essential Wendell Berry*

Daniel Levin, *Nothing but a Circus: Misadventures among the Powerful*

Stephen Church, *Henry III: A Simple and God-Fearing King*

Pankaj Mishra, *Age of Anger: A History of the Present*

Graeme Wood, *The Way of the Strangers: Encounters with the Islamic State*

Michael Lewis, *The Undoing Project: A Friendship that Changed the World*

John Romer, *A History of Ancient Egypt, Volume 2: From the Great Pyramid to the Fall of the Middle Kingdom*

Andy King, *Edward I: A New King Arthur?*

Thomas L. Friedman, *Thank You for Being Late: An Optimist's Guide to Thriving in the Age of Accelerations*

John Edwards, *Mary I: The Daughter of Time*

Grayson Perry, *The Descent of Man*

Deyan Sudjic, *The Language of Cities*

Norman Ohler, *Blitzed: Drugs in Nazi Germany*

Carlo Rovelli, *Reality Is Not What It Seems: The Journey to Quantum Gravity*

Catherine Merridale, *Lenin on the Train*

Susan Greenfield, *A Day in the Life of the Brain: The Neuroscience of Consciousness from Dawn Till Dusk*

Christopher Given-Wilson, *Edward II: The Terrors of Kingship*

Emma Jane Kirby, *The Optician of Lampedusa*

Minoo Dinshaw, *Outlandish Knight: The Byzantine Life of Steven Runciman*

Candice Millard, *Hero of the Empire: The Making of Winston Churchill*

Christopher de Hamel, *Meetings with Remarkable Manuscripts*

Brian Cox and Jeff Forshaw, *Universal: A Guide to the Cosmos*

Ryan Avent, *The Wealth of Humans: Work and Its Absence in the Twenty-first Century*

Jodie Archer and Matthew L. Jockers, *The Bestseller Code*

Cathy O'Neil, *Weapons of Math Destruction: How Big Data Increases Inequality and Threatens Democracy*

Peter Wadhams, *A Farewell to Ice: A Report from the Arctic*

Richard J. Evans, *The Pursuit of Power: Europe, 1815-1914*

Anthony Gottlieb, *The Dream of Enlightenment: The Rise of Modern Philosophy*

Frank Trentmann, *Empire of Things: How We Became a World of Consumers, from the Fifteenth Century to the Twenty-First*

Laura Ashe, *Richard II: A Brittle Glory*

John Donvan and Caren Zucker, *In a Different Key: The Story of Autism*

Jack Shenker, *The Egyptians: A Radical Story*

Tim Judah, *In Wartime: Stories from Ukraine*

Serhii Plokhy, *The Gates of Europe: A History of Ukraine*

Robin Lane Fox, *Augustine: Conversions and Confessions*

Peter Hennessy and James Jinks, *The Silent Deep: The Royal Navy Submarine Service Since 1945*

Seán McMeekin, *The Ottoman Endgame: War, Revolution and the Making of the Modern Middle East, 1908–1923*

Charles Moore, *Margaret Thatcher: The Authorized Biography, Volume Two: Everything She Wants*

Dominic Sandbrook, *The Great British Dream Factory: The Strange History of Our National Imagination*

Larissa MacFarquhar, *Strangers Drowning: Voyages to the Brink of Moral Extremity*

Niall Ferguson, *Kissinger: 1923-1968: The Idealist*

Carlo Rovelli, *Seven Brief Lessons on Physics*

Tim Blanning, *Frederick the Great: King of Prussia*

Ian Kershaw, *To Hell and Back: Europe, 1914–1949*

Pedro Domingos, *The Master Algorithm: How the Quest for the Ultimate Learning Machine Will Remake Our World*

David Wootton, *The Invention of Science: A New History of the Scientific Revolution*

Christopher Tyerman, *How to Plan a Crusade: Reason and Religious War in the Middle Ages*

Andy Beckett, *Promised You A Miracle: UK 80–82*

Carl Watkins, *Stephen: The Reign of Anarchy*

Anne Curry, *Henry V: From Playboy Prince to Warrior King*

John Gillingham, *William II: The Red King*

Roger Knight, *William IV: A King at Sea*

Douglas Hurd, *Elizabeth II: The Steadfast*

Richard Nisbett, *Mindware: Tools for Smart Thinking*

Jochen Bleicken, *Augustus: The Biography*

Paul Mason, *PostCapitalism: A Guide to Our Future*

Frank Wilczek, *A Beautiful Question: Finding Nature's Deep Design*

Roberto Saviano, *Zero Zero Zero*

Owen Hatherley, *Landscapes of Communism: A History Through Buildings*

César Hidalgo, *Why Information Grows: The Evolution of Order, from Atoms to Economies*

Aziz Ansari and Eric Klinenberg, *Modern Romance: An Investigation*

Sudhir Hazareesingh, *How the French Think: An Affectionate Portrait of an Intellectual People*

Steven D. Levitt and Stephen J. Dubner, *When to Rob a Bank: A Rogue Economist's Guide to the World*

Leonard Mlodinow, *The Upright Thinkers: The Human Journey from Living in Trees to Understanding the Cosmos*

Hans Ulrich Obrist, *Lives of the Artists, Lives of the Architects*

Richard H. Thaler, *Misbehaving: The Making of Behavioural Economics*

Sheldon Solomon, Jeff Greenberg and Tom Pyszczynski, *Worm at the Core: On the Role of Death in Life*

Nathaniel Popper, *Digital Gold: The Untold Story of Bitcoin*

Dominic Lieven, *Towards the Flame: Empire, War and the End of Tsarist Russia*

Noel Malcolm, *Agents of Empire: Knights, Corsairs, Jesuits and Spies in the Sixteenth-Century Mediterranean World*

James Rebanks, *The Shepherd's Life: A Tale of the Lake District*

David Brooks, *The Road to Character*

Joseph Stiglitz, *The Great Divide*

Ken Robinson and Lou Aronica, *Creative Schools: Revolutionizing Education from the Ground Up*

Clotaire Rapaille and Andrés Roemer, *Move UP: Why Some Cultures Advances While Others Don't*

Jonathan Keates, *William III and Mary II: Partners in Revolution*

David Womersley, *James II: The Last Catholic King*

Richard Barber, *Henry II: A Prince Among Princes*

Jane Ridley, *Victoria: Queen, Matriarch, Empress*

John Gray, *The Soul of the Marionette: A Short Enquiry into Human Freedom*

Emily Wilson, *Seneca: A Life*

Michael Barber, *How to Run a Government: So That Citizens Benefit and Taxpayers Don't Go Crazy*

Dana Thomas, *Gods and Kings: The Rise and Fall of Alexander McQueen and John Galliano*

Steven Weinberg, *To Explain the World: The Discovery of Modern Science*

Jennifer Jacquet, *Is Shame Necessary?: New Uses for an Old Tool*

Eugene Rogan, *The Fall of the Ottomans: The Great War in the Middle East, 1914-1920*

Norman Doidge, *The Brain's Way of Healing: Stories of Remarkable Recoveries and Discoveries*

John Hooper, *The Italians*

Sven Beckert, *Empire of Cotton: A New History of Global Capitalism*

Mark Kishlansky, *Charles I: An Abbreviated Life*

Philip Ziegler, *George VI: The Dutiful King*

David Cannadine, *George V: The Unexpected King*

Stephen Alford, *Edward VI: The Last Boy King*

John Guy, *Henry VIII: The Quest for Fame*

Robert Tombs, *The English and their History: The First Thirteen Centuries*

Neil MacGregor, *Germany: The Memories of a Nation*

Uwe Tellkamp, *The Tower: A Novel*

Roberto Calasso, *Ardor*

Slavoj Žižek, *Trouble in Paradise: Communism After the End of History*

Francis Pryor, *Home: A Time Traveller's Tales from Britain's Prehistory*

R. F. Foster, *Vivid Faces: The Revolutionary Generation in Ireland, 1890-1923*

Andrew Roberts, *Napoleon the Great*

Shami Chakrabarti, *On Liberty*

Bessel van der Kolk, *The Body Keeps the Score: Mind, Brain and Body in the Transformation of Trauma*

Brendan Simms, *The Longest Afternoon: The 400 Men Who Decided the Battle of Waterloo*

Naomi Klein, *This Changes Everything: Capitalism vs the Climate*

Owen Jones, *The Establishment: And How They Get Away with It*

Caleb Scharf, *The Copernicus Complex: Our Cosmic Significance in a Universe of Planets and Probabilities*

Martin Wolf, *The Shifts and the Shocks: What We've Learned - and Have Still to Learn - from the Financial Crisis*

Steven Pinker, *The Sense of Style: The Thinking Person's Guide to Writing in the 21st Century*

Vincent Deary, *How We Are: Book One of the How to Live Trilogy*

Henry Kissinger, *World Order*

Alexander Watson, *Ring of Steel: Germany and Austria-Hungary at War, 1914-1918*

PENGUIN BOOKS
Edward VIII

Piers Brendon is the author of over a dozen books, among them *The Dark Valley: A Panorama of the 1930s* and *The Decline and Fall of the British Empire*. Formerly Keeper of the Churchill Archives Centre, he is a Fellow of Churchill College, Cambridge, and a Fellow of the Royal Society of Literature.